D1156424

The Weimar Republic and the Rise of Fascism

Brett Griffin

Cavendish Square
New York

Published in 2018 by Cavendish Square Publishing, LLC
243 5th Avenue, Suite 136, New York, NY 10016

First Edition

Website: cavendishsq.com

CPSIA Compliance Information: Batch #CS17CSQ

Library of Congress Cataloging-in-Publication Data

Names: Griffin, Brett, author.
Title: The Weimar Republic and the rise of fascism / Brett Griffin.
Description: New York : Cavendish Square Publishing, [2018] |
Series: The interwar years | Includes bibliographical references and index.
Identifiers: LCCN 2017002479 (print) | LCCN 2017003057 (ebook) |
ISBN 9781502627186 (library bound) | ISBN 9781502627179 (E-book)
Subjects: LCSH: Germany--Politics and government--1918-1933. | National socialism.
Classification: LCC DD240 .G75 2018 (print) | LCC DD240 (ebook) | DDC 943.085--dc23
LC record available at https://lccn.loc.gov/2017002479

Editorial Director: David McNamara
Editor: Kristen Susienka
Copy Editor: Alex Tessman
Associate Art Director: Amy Greenan
Designer: Alan Sliwinski
Production Coordinator: Karol Szymczuk
Photo Research: J8 Media

The photographs in this book are used by permission and through the courtesy of: Cover, pp. 1, 2 Print Collector/Hulton Archive/Getty Images; Background images used throughout book, James Weston/Shutterstock.com; Supermimicry/Shutterstock.com; pp. 4, 10, 34 Bettmann/Getty Images; p. 8 frmir, own work/File: Emperor Wilhelm2.jpg/Wikimedia Commons; pp. 14, 62, 75 Ullstein Bild/Getty Images; p. 18 APIC/Getty Images; p. 19 Boury/Three Lions/Hulton Archive/Getty Images; p. 29 Albert Harlingue/Roger Viollet/Getty Images; p. 32 Estate of Emil Bieber/Klaus Niermann/Getty Images; p. 39 Photographer unknown/File: Bundesarchiv Bild 183-1989-0322-506, Adolf Hitler, Kinderbild.jpg/Wikimedia Commons; pp. 49, 78 , 91 Universal History Archive/Getty images; p. 51 Hulton Archive/Getty Images; p. 58 Hulton-Deutsch Collection/Corbis/Getty Images; p. 68 Buyenlarge/Getty Images; p. 70 Movie Poster Image Art/Getty Images; p. 80 Rolls Press/Popperfoto/Getty Images; p. 82 European/FPG/Archive Photos/Getty Images; p. 90 Hulton-Deutsch Collection/Corbis/Getty Images; p. 98 John Moore/Getty Images; p. 105 Erik McGregor/Pacific Press/LightRocket/Getty Images; p. 112 Nicolas Koutsokostas/Corbis/Getty Images.

Printed in the United States of America

Contents

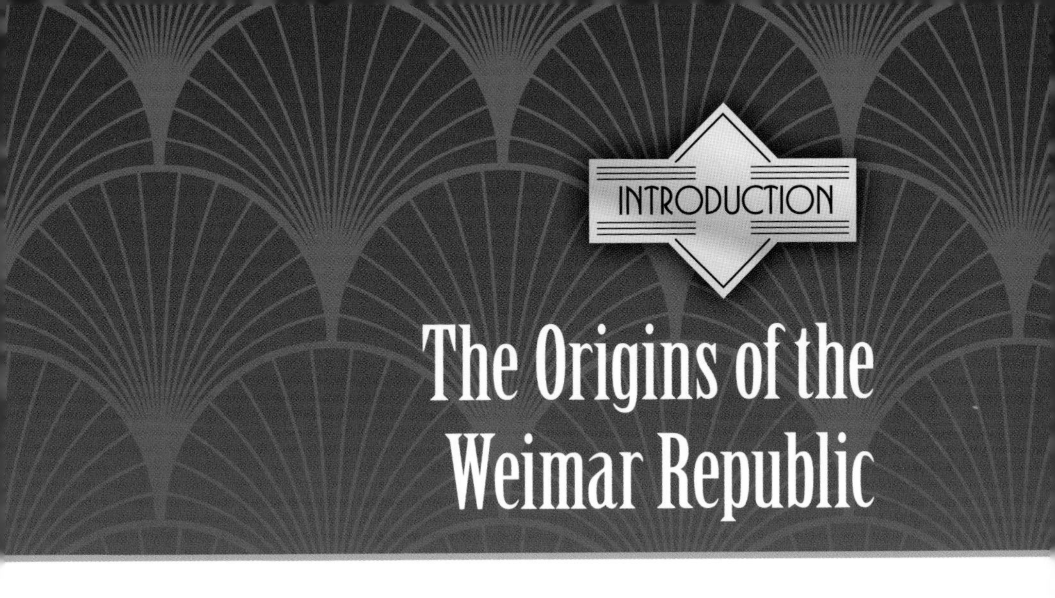

INTRODUCTION

The Origins of the Weimar Republic

The end of World War I on November 11, 1918, marked a turning point in world history. The old political and social order in Europe was dead, the war having resulted in the destruction of the four imperial regimes that had controlled most of the lands and peoples of the continent. Britain and France were left as the two primary European powers, and the Paris Peace Conference of 1919 marked the first major involvement of the United States in European affairs. It was Germany, however, whose political, economic, and social structures were most disrupted by the end of the war, and whose struggles over the next two decades would ultimately embroil the world in a global conflict for the second time in half a century.

Opposite: *German soldiers operate a machine gun in the trenches of World War I, the conflict that brought an end to the German Empire.*

Weimar

The short-lived Weimar Republic, the parliamentary democracy established in Germany in 1919 that ultimately fell to Adolf Hitler and the Nazis in 1933, is now remembered largely for its tragic, ignominious end. The word "Weimar" has come to be synonymous with political failure and paralysis in the face of great evil, and Weimar's legacy is often invoked as a dire warning. The failings of the Weimar government and its leaders were many, but the fall of the republic reaches truly Shakespearian levels of tragedy when viewed in the hopeful context in which it was formed. Obscured by the sheer scale of the devastation that followed the destruction of Weimar is the hope and promise of Germany in the 1920s, when the country was a burgeoning democracy characterized by political freedom and one of the richest cultures in all of interwar Europe. The journey from hope and progress to despair and **Fascism** is the true story of Weimar Germany, one that continues to echo with ominous warnings to this day.

The democratic government that was to eventually become the Weimar Republic was formed in response to Germany's failing fortunes in World War I. Conditions on the home front had deteriorated throughout the war, mirroring the German army's declining success on the battlefield. By 1918, food rationing was in full effect across Germany, and shortages of wheat and rye resulted in bread being made with sawdust. Women, even those employed in jobs that had been vacated by the men at the front, still struggled to provide for their families. Meanwhile, 2 million German men died fighting the war, and another 4.2 million were wounded. These casualties amounted to a staggering 19 percent of the entire male population of Germany, and the effects of this culling of the population were felt for years after the armistice. Wounded veterans, sporting scars or missing limbs, were a common sight in postwar Germany, and many soldiers suffered from post-traumatic stress disorder (PTSD), or "shell shock," and struggled to readjust to peacetime society as a result. For families whose sons or husbands or fathers never returned from the trenches, replacing the lost wages of their late loved ones became a titanic struggle. This problem was exacerbated when those women who were now the primary breadwinners for their families found themselves turned out of their jobs to make room for soldiers returning from the front.

Still, for all the hardships presented by the war, there was a degree of liberation that went along with it. Women were employed in greater numbers than ever before and now had money that was theirs to control. While this may have proved to be cold comfort to a woman struggling to prevent her family from starving, it at least signified that things could change, and that women could live independently of the men in their families. More important to the immediate postwar environment was the loss of faith in authority and elite institutions. As the German government, led by **Kaiser** (or Emperor) Wilhelm II, and the German army, under the command of Field Marshal Paul von Hindenburg

This painting shows Kaiser Wilhelm II. His abdication allowed for the creation of the Weimar Republic.

and General Erich Ludendorff, failed to break through the trenches of France, public trust in their ability to properly prosecute the war waned. With no end to the fighting in sight and increasing food shortages at home, the German people began to question the competence and the interests of those in positions of authority. Did they really know what they were doing? Did they have the German peoples' interest at heart? If not, whose interests were they serving? The patriotic fervor that had greeted the war in 1914 had turned to bitterness and disillusionment by 1918.

The German Revolution

Fully aware of this shift in public opinion, and with troops depleted and the army running low on material resources, Hindenburg and Ludendorff requested an armistice of Kaiser Wilhelm II on September 29, 1918. After some debate, the kaiser determined that Germany's best hope for a just peace settlement would be with the Americans. President Woodrow Wilson had spent the past year declaring his hope for a "peace without victory" and promoting his Fourteen Points, an idealistic vision of a postwar Europe characterized by self-determination, international cooperation, and an end to war. Trusting that Wilson would live up to his word, the kaiser initiated democratizing reforms to his own government, as a show of good faith. Maximilian von Baden was appointed chancellor, and a new government was formed within the Reichstag, the German parliament. Germany was made into a constitutional monarchy more answerable to the Reichstag than to the kaiser, but it was not enough for the Americans, or for the German people.

On October 29, 1918, in the port city of Kiel, a group of sailors mutinied, refusing to return to service. Soon, the entire city had risen in support, calling for an end to the war and

A crowd of thousands gathers outside of the Reichstag building to hear the news of the kaiser's abdication.

the abdication of the kaiser. Like a spark in dry brush, the events of Kiel ignited the German population in a rejection of the imperial regime. In city after city, soldiers mutinied, workers rebelled, and local governments were toppled. In their place were formed councils, groups of workers and/or soldiers coming together to direct local affairs themselves. Modeled on the Bolshevik councils that had formed in revolutionary Russia a year earlier, the councils of revolutionary Germany allowed for an unprecedented degree of direct democracy. They called for not only the abdication of the kaiser but the formation of a truly democratic government, electoral and social reforms, and an end to the **militarism** that had been a matter of policy for Germany since the days of Otto von Bismarck. Some of the councils saw themselves as mere placeholders, a provisional government charged with maintaining order until a proper election could be called, while others took more direct action, actively working to replace local officials and initiate change at the local level.

Becoming a Republic

The revolutionary fervor proved to be more than the existing government could handle. On November 9, 1918, Maximilian von Baden announced that the kaiser had abdicated his throne, shortly before resigning himself and passing the chancellorship to Friedrich Ebert, the leader of the Social Democratic Party (SPD). That afternoon, one of Ebert's deputies declared from a balcony of the Reichstag building that Germany was now a republic.

Meanwhile, from the balcony of a separate building, Communist leader Karl Liebknecht declared that Germany was now a "Free Socialist Republic," to be modeled after the Bolshevik government in Russia. Despite the confusion over which form the new German government would take, one thing was clear: the revolution had been successful. The kaiser had been removed from power, and Germany would have a government that would respond to the people. Democracy had prevailed, and the days of living under an autocratic ruler with absolute power were over.

Unfortunately, that state of affairs would prove tragically short-lived. In less than fifteen years, Germany would once again be under the heel of a dictatorship, the promise of the revolution broken. The Weimar Republic faced problems from its very inception. Multiple parties with radically different ideas about what kind of government should be put in place competed for power in the Reichstag, the economy suffered from both runaway inflation and the Great Depression in the same decade, and the Treaty of Versailles humiliated Germany and imposed harsh terms on the country. This environment led to the rise of the Nazi Party under Adolf Hitler. Animated by extreme **nationalism** and **anti-Semitism**, the Nazis were able to take advantage of the crisis that resulted from the Great Depression and the political gridlock that followed. Upon their coming to power in 1933, the idea of a free, democratic Germany was dead. Opposition parties were outlawed, intellectuals, scientists, and artists fled, and what had once been a vibrant political and cultural scene turned into a graveyard for democracy, art, and higher learning. Having crushed the republic, Hitler was now free to pursue his goals of territorial expansion and racial purification, leading directly to World War II and the Holocaust.

Legacies and Lessons

It is important to understand the context of these events and the reasons that they came about. The legacy of the Nazis,

World War II, and the Holocaust continues to haunt the world today, and though Hitler may be a figure of the past, his ideology and the hatred he espoused remain relevant. Aggressive nationalism, demonization of those deemed outsiders, and hostility to a genuinely free and open society all have direct parallels with modern political movements. Modern Fascists may not be waving banners adorned with swastikas or arguing for the construction of concentration camps, but they do push for policies that are at their core discriminatory and aimed at marginalizing and excluding people of certain races, religions, and ethnicities from active participation in society. For those who wish to resist these policies—for those who believe in democracy, freedom, diversity, equality, and justice—the lessons of Weimar Germany must be learned and internalized lest the same mistakes be made again.

1 The Weimar Republic

Upon the abdication of Kaiser Wilhelm II on November 9, 1918, both Friedrich Ebert's Social Democrats (SPD) and Karl Liebknecht's Communists (eventually organized into the Communist Party, or KPD) proclaimed German republics. While both parties had different conceptions of how the new government should be organized, there was at least general agreement on the need for democracy and social reforms, and hope for the future. Within a little over two months, however, Liebknecht would be dead, murdered by forces working at the behest of Ebert's government, and the new Weimar **coalition** would be turning to its bitterest enemies in an effort to maintain control of Germany.

Opposite: *From a balcony of the Reichstag building, Germany is declared a republic by Philipp Scheidemann of the Social Democratic Party (SPD).*

Starting Out

The early months of the Weimar Republic are indicative of the fatal flaw at the heart of the fledgling democracy. The collapse of the kaiser's imperial regime had given rise to an unprecedented flowering of political thought. Students, workers, women, and soldiers returning home from the war all took an active role in politics for the first time and made their voices heard. The sheer variety of opinions, however, made it difficult for any government to form that could appeal to even a bare majority of the people. The political left was made up of Communists, Social Democrats, and liberals, while the right consisted of conservatives, monarchists, autocrats, and, eventually, the Nazis. All of these groups had fundamentally different ideas regarding what kind of government should be established and whom that government should serve. **Communism** held that society should be organized in such a way as to deliver the means of production to the workers, eliminating class boundaries and free markets. **Social democracy** pushed to have certain services provided by the state and the economy closely regulated, but it did not argue for the elimination of all markets or the institution of full Communism. Meanwhile, many parties of the right did not even believe in democracy as an institution, and instead wanted to return to some form of dictatorship. The incompatibility of these competing visions of government would ultimately lead to disaster for the republic.

Chaos and Compromise

In the beginning, it was Ebert's SPD that succeeded in forming the first functional government for the newly democratic Germany, on November 11, 1918. By allying with the Independent Social Democratic Party (USPD), Ebert was able to form a coalition that was large enough to hold a majority of seats in the Reichstag, and the new government set about immediately passing democratic reforms. Freedoms of speech, religion, and press were quickly established, and women were granted the right to vote. World War I had also been ended, a key demand of the revolutionaries, with the new government complying with the Americans' terms for surrender. This infuriated the German military, a conservative institution that still felt loyalty to the kaiser and to the militaristic tradition of imperial Germany. To deflect blame, many within the army's ranks insisted that the country had been betrayed from within, and that the new government had robbed Germany of its victory by cowardly surrendering to the Allies. Marxists and socialists were often accused of being the "traitors" responsible for Germany's defeat, but by far the most common target of this allegation was the Jewish population. The myth that the country had been "stabbed in the back" by the Jews in World War I was a powerful salve for those who felt humiliated by Germany's defeat, and one that gained traction in the years that followed.

With the war over, soldiers returned home in droves. The decommissioning of the military proceeded in a somewhat

Friedrich Ebert, circa 1920

disorganized fashion, with many soldiers managing to hang onto their weapons. At the same time, munitions factories, no longer needed, closed their doors. The workers who had lost their jobs joined the returning soldiers in seeking employment, producing a large population of dislocated citizens. Some joined the councils and demonstrations sweeping the country in the weeks following the war's end. Others, struggling to adapt to life outside of the trenches, took the military weapons and equipment they still possessed and joined **paramilitary** formations. These independent, loosely organized armies roamed throughout the country acting as private mercenaries for political parties or private actors. Right-wing paramilitaries used violence to enforce and maintain order in the cities while terrorizing peasants and Jews in the countryside.

In the face of Germany's newly opened, unruly society, Friedrich Ebert's main priorities were maintaining stability and getting the new government on its feet. Ebert, though he instituted many social democratic reforms, did not want to follow Russia's example and become a Communist state; he feared that the economic chaos and political terror that had plagued Russia in the year since its revolution would replicate itself in Germany if such a thing were attempted.

This angered the Communists, who believed that there would never be a better time to establish a Marxist state than the present, before the new constitution had even been written.

Sensing that Ebert and the SPD were not allies in this fight, Liebknecht and Rosa Luxemberg, the cofounders of the KPD, led a revolt. Consisting of a general strike and demonstrations against the SPD-led government, the uprising seemed to confirm Ebert's worst fears. To his mind, public order was threatened, the faith of the people in the new government was potentially in jeopardy, and a full-scale Bolshevik revolution could break out.

As a result, compromises were sought with those most opposed to the republic from the right, in order to prevent what Ebert perceived to be a significant challenge to the government from the left. The military agreed to crush the revolt, as long as the SPD would not interfere with the army's central structure or heap dishonor upon the institution or

Karl Liebknecht, the cofounder of the German Communist Party (KPD), gives a fiery address in 1918.

its officials. To mollify those citizens that might otherwise be sympathetic to the Communists, the SPD struck a deal with business owners and industrialists: employers agreed to establish an eight-hour workday and permit workers to form unions in exchange for the government's vow to respect the rights of private capital by not moving to nationalize private industry. These compromises directly contradicted the wishes of not only the Communists but also the broader left. The military and the class of business owners and industrial magnates were among those that had benefitted most from the rule of the kaiser, and a major goal of the left had been to strip these individuals of their power and influence over the new republic, thus ensuring the country would not drift back into the militant autocracy of imperial Germany. By empowering these figures and promising not to strip them of rank, prestige, or privilege, Ebert and the SPD allowed the elites of the old Germany to remain the elites of the new Germany. These elites were hostile to the very idea of democracy and would spend most of the next decade scheming to undermine the republic in any way possible.

In the short term, Ebert's compromise worked. The Communist revolt was brutally crushed, as were others like it. Liebknecht and Luxemburg were captured by a paramilitary unit and subsequently detained, interrogated, tortured, and executed. Order was maintained, and in early 1919 a new constitution was drafted in the city of Weimar. The Weimar Constitution formalized the new republic, and the first official coalition government was formed between the SPD and other parties of the moderate left and center. Ebert was elected president, a position that was responsible for selecting the chancellor and the cabinet, and which was invested with the power to allow the chancellor to govern by decree in times of emergency. The constitution formally guaranteed the political freedoms that had been granted in the first days of the revolution, established a system of unemployment insurance, and codified the promises made by the business elites that they would recognize workers' rights.

In the long term, however, the circumstances surrounding the founding of the republic would also sow the seeds for its destruction. For many workers and members of the left, the promise of the revolution had already been broken. The fear of a Communist uprising had caused the SPD to seek compromise with the parties and figures of the right, driving a permanent wedge between the Communists and the Social Democrats and splitting the overall left-wing opposition to the policies pursued by the right. In addition to this split, the compromises made by Ebert empowered the elites in the military, bureaucracy, and private sector, allowing them to continue exerting outside influence over the political process. Once the immediate crisis of the Communist revolt was over, these elite figures abandoned the SPD and began funding and supporting the parties of the far right, particularly the German National People's Party (DNVP), an openly anti-Semitic, militaristic party that longed for a return to the time of the kaiser. The failure to break the control these fundamentally anti-democratic elites held over large parts of German society would come back to haunt the SPD in the last years of the Weimar Republic.

Signing the Treaty

While Germany was struggling internally to establish a new government, other forces were also concerning themselves with the future of the country. In Paris, the leaders of the world's great powers were meeting for the Peace Conference that would bring World War I to a formal close and determine the fate of the defeated parties. The nations that had emerged victorious held complete control over the terms of the peace, while Germany and the other defeated participants were not even given a seat at the negotiating table. When German representatives were finally invited, their train crawled through the devastated French countryside on its way to Paris, forcing the delegates to take in the full scale of the destruction wreaked by the German army. The delegates' hopes that Germany would be treated fairly by the victorious Allies waned with every mile.

Those hopes were dashed altogether when the German representatives saw the terms of the Treaty of Versailles. Germany was to lose one-seventh of its territory, with various lands being transferred to France, Denmark, and the newly formed nations of Poland and Czechoslovakia. Germany was also stripped of its overseas colonies, and diplomatic and trade agreements with foreign countries were canceled. To further prevent German involvement in international affairs, the nation was denied entrance to the League of Nations.

THE PRIMARY POLITICAL PARTIES OF WEIMAR GERMANY

Communist Party (KPD) Founded by Karl Liebknecht and Rosa Luxemburg, the Communists pushed for a transition to a Russian-style Soviet republic. They were fully committed to Marxism and the notion of a class struggle aimed at delivering the means of production to the workers. As a result, the core constituency of the KPD was the German working class, particularly after the Great Depression.

Social Democratic Party (SPD) The most prominent left-wing party in Weimar Germany, the SPD believed in social democracy and fought for the rights of workers, but it did not push for the full implementation of Communism. The SPD did succeed in passing numerous reforms, including an unemployment insurance program, an overhaul of the welfare system, guarantees of workers' collective bargaining power, and women's suffrage.

German National People's Party (DNVP) A right-wing party, the DNVP represented the interests of the upper classes, the military, and business owners. Openly authoritarian, the DNVP idolized the military and wanted to see Germany recover the lands and glory it had lost in World War I. The DNVP was extremely nationalistic, and blamed Jews and other "foreign elements" for many of the problems faced by Germany.

National Socialist German Worker's Party (NSDAP) Also known as the Nazis, the NSDAP, under Adolf Hitler's leadership, came to rule Germany in 1933 as a one-party dictatorship. Wedding aggressive nationalism with militant anti-Semitism and anti-Marxism, the Nazis were a Fascist party that, despite their irrelevance for most of the 1920s, ultimately succeeded in destroying the Weimar Republic.

Beyond the loss of territory and international prestige, Germany was also fundamentally changed internally. The military was limited to one hundred thousand men, most military equipment was to be confiscated, and the establishment of an air force was forbidden. Strict limits were placed on the numbers and types of weapons that Germany was allowed to maintain, and the draft was outlawed.

The most galling term to the German people was Article 231, the war guilt clause, which forced Germany to accept full responsibility and blame for all damages incurred during the war. As a direct consequence of accepting this blame, Germany would be forced to pay an unspecified amount in **reparations**. The eventual amount of these reparations was to be determined separately, by a special commission. The German delegates were stunned by the harshness of these terms and tried to renegotiate them, but to no avail—the Allies refused to consider any counterproposals. Faced with a choice of signing the treaty or suffering an invasion of Germany by the Allies, the Treaty of Versailles was signed on June 28, 1919.

Reactions, Reparations, and Inflation

Within Germany, reaction to the treaty was overwhelmingly negative. Germans of all political persuasions were outraged at the terms, viewing them as a "thumb in the eye" or, as Hitler eventually termed it, "highway robbery." The loss of territory and the war guilt clause were humiliating, and the suppression of the military, historically an incredibly important part of German culture, proved especially infuriating to many on the right. The belief that Germany had been sold out or "stabbed in the back" during the war only intensified after the Treaty of Versailles, its terms upheld as proof that internal enemies had conspired with the Allies to weaken Germany. The right used this myth as a cudgel against their political opponents, claiming that the Weimar coalition was made up of socialists, Marxists, and Jews, and that they had colluded with the enemy by signing this treaty.

The reparations payments demanded by the Treaty of Versailles were also seen as an excessively harsh punishment, and the state of the German economy did not inspire confidence that they could be met. The immediate postwar economy was characterized by **inflation**. When prices rose, the purchasing power of German currency fell, as each monetary unit was worth less in the context of the overall economy. The inflation was at first caused by the sale of war bonds during World War I. Confident that Germany would prevail on the battlefield, the kaiser had borrowed heavily from the citizenry to finance the war, assuming that the gain in material resources in conquered territories would allow the government to easily repay the bonds. Upon Germany's defeat, however, the new Weimar Republic found itself saddled with a large war debt that necessitated the bulk printing of money to pay off. The subsequent increase in the supply of the mark—the basic unit of German currency—led to an increase in prices, beginning a cycle of spiraling inflation.

The inflation worsened once the reparations bill was delivered. The commission tasked with determining the amount that Germany would be required to pay announced its terms on May 5, 1921: a total of 132 billion marks, with 2 billion due every year, in addition to the value of 26 percent of German exports; this sum was to be paid in hard currency (i.e. gold) rather than paper marks.

The Weimar government pleaded with the commission in London, desperately trying to renegotiate the terms. While the German economy had begun to improve, the payments were still going to be nearly impossible to make. The commission steadfastly refused to adjust the bill in Germany's favor, leaving the Weimar leadership with few options. Ultimately, more paper marks were printed in order to purchase hard currency that could be used to pay the first installment of the reparations. As more paper marks were printed, however, inflation rose.

In addition to the crisis posed by the reparations payments, Germany was also facing a problem with labor. The immediate postwar inflation had stimulated investment from business leaders, and it was partly for this reason that the German economy did not suffer more greatly from the rise in prices. Goods and services may have been more costly, but unemployment remained relatively low in the first few years of the republic. By the early 1920s, however, workers were beginning to strike for wage increases, to keep pace with the rise in the cost of living. These wage increases were granted through the printing of more money. This in turn led to further inflation, and further strikes, and the printing of yet more money. As this cycle continued, inflation turned into **hyperinflation** by 1922. Businesses were now starting to feel the effects of the crisis, and unemployment rose. More money was then printed to meet the costs of the unemployment insurance program, and businesses were subsidized to help keep them afloat. These policies only made the hyperinflation worse.

By 1923, the collectors of Germany's war reparations began to grow nervous about the state of the German economy, as well as suspicious of the Weimar leadership. Believing that the German government might be intentionally sabotaging its economy in an effort to dodge reparations payments, French and Belgian officials decided to invade and personally administer the Ruhr valley in January. The Ruhr, located in northwestern Germany, was the industrial heartland of the country, and the French and Belgian governments agreed to extract what they were owed in reparations from the region.

In response to this invasion by foreign powers, the Weimar government urged "passive resistance" on the part of the workers in the Ruhr. Rather than suffering the indignity of being forced to work by a foreign military, workers were instructed to walk off the job and shut the factories down. The workers complied with this program, and the productivity of the Ruhr ground to a halt. Unfortunately, shutting down one of the most financially and industrially important regions of the country did not help the ailing economy. In fact, the hyperinflation crisis was made far worse, as the government was forced to compensate both the resisting workers and the business owners whose factories were sitting idle.

The hyperinflation reached its peak at the end of 1923. A 100 trillion mark note was issued in November, at which point the exchange rate stood at an utterly staggering 1 US dollar to 4.2 trillion marks. For the German people, this crisis was devastating. Life savings were wiped out overnight as the currency became increasingly worthless, and the bare necessities of life became prohibitively expensive. Families had to decide which bills to pay, and class boundaries evaporated as once well-to-do Germans found themselves waiting in bread lines with members of the lower classes. People stripped apart fences for firewood and found themselves pushing wheelbarrows full of cash to the market to buy a single loaf of bread. Those fortunate enough to possess a bit of foreign currency suddenly found themselves among the wealthiest people in the country, and could count themselves among the few to benefit from the crisis.

Taking Action

With the economic situation growing increasingly dire and the populace becoming more desperate by the day, the government was forced to act. Negotiations with France and Belgium were opened in September to attempt to end the standoff in the Ruhr and find a resolution to the economic crisis. Business leaders were invited into the discussions, and they took advantage of the opportunity to roll back several

German children use devalued marks as scrap paper during the height of the hyperinflation crisis.

of the protections for workers that had been guaranteed by the Weimar Republic.

Under the auspices of these changes being necessary for the health of the economy, the largely conservative private interests successfully ended the eight-hour workday, cut the social welfare system, and scaled back many of the business regulations that were negatively affecting their profits. A new currency, the Rentenmark, was established, which served to stabilize the economy and end the hyperinflation in one stroke. However, this resulted in the previous currency becoming utterly worthless—for instance, one trillion paper marks could be exchanged for one Rentenmark. Finally, the schedule for reparations payments was adjusted, allowing Germany to more easily meet its obligations. The French and Belgian governments agreed to withdraw their troops from the Ruhr, and the Dawes Plan of 1924 finalized the new payment schedule.

Though the inflationary crisis was resolved, it was not without consequence. The reparations continued to be a political weapon deployed against the SPD, even after they ceased to be an economic problem. These attacks from the right began to attract a wider range of receptive listeners. The initial inflation had soured the middle class on the SPD and its coalition partners, and their votes began going to more right-wing parties. The working class reacted much more negatively to the stabilization process, as workers were forced to bear most of the burden of the new economic policies, losing many of their benefits and having to work longer hours. Workers began drifting toward the KPD and other left-wing parties, leaving the SPD and the parties of the center with a steadily dwindling base of support. Beginning in 1924, control of the Reichstag was passed to the right.

The Great Depression Begins

With the economy back under control, the Weimar Republic entered a period of stability and growing prosperity during the mid-1920s. The Rentenmark was replaced with the Reichsmark in the fall of 1924, a currency on the gold standard, and this stability stimulated a wave of foreign—particularly American—investment. With capital pouring into the country, German businesses flourished and public consumption soared. A system of rationalization came to industry, a process by which supposedly scientific methods would be used to increase output while decreasing labor, thereby maximizing profits. By 1927, the economy had fully recovered and industrial output was back to its prewar levels. The gains were spread to the working class, as the government began to shorten the workday, raised wages, and reinstated the unemployment insurance program. The 1928 elections restored the SPD to power, and the parties of the far right were marginalized. The young republic, having survived major crises in its first years, was now in a position of relative comfort and seemed poised to continue in a hopeful, prosperous direction. Then disaster struck.

The Great Depression, which began in the United States in October 1929, proved devastating to the Weimar Republic. When the American economy crashed, US-based bankers called in their loans, including those that had been made to the German business community. The same investments that had allowed German industry to prosper now brought the country to its knees, as those who had received loans ran out of money trying to pay them back all at once. Mass layoffs followed, and many businesses shut down entirely. The unemployment rate soared, and by 1932 six million Germans—one-third of the labor force—were out of work. To make matters worse, the government found itself incapable of dealing with the crisis. The unemployment insurance program, newly restored in 1927, was never intended to deal with joblessness on the scale that was now seen. Overwhelmed, the program went bankrupt in less than a year. The Reichstag descended into gridlock, unable to decide what to do next and becoming utterly paralyzed. The government spending that would later

PRESIDENT PAUL VON HINDENBURG

Serving as the German president from 1925 to 1934, Paul von Hindenburg was a beloved figure in his time, but in the years since, he has gone down in history as the man who gave power to Adolf Hitler. Born on October 2, 1847, to an aristocratic Prussian family, Hindenburg led a distinguished military career during the second half of the nineteenth century, upholding the traditional Prussian values of loyalty, honor, and obedience. As leader of German forces in World War I, he quickly became known as the victor of Tannenberg following his smashing success in an early engagement.

After the death of Friedrich Ebert in 1925, Hindenburg was elected president by a slim plurality of votes. He remained popular across all segments of German society but was particularly supported by the right. A monarchist and German nationalist at heart, Hindenburg never fully believed in the republic, though he would listen to the counsel of those around him. Gustav Stresemann, foreign minister at the time of Hindenburg's election, warned that the "main thing is [to ensure] that uncontrollable people do not gain influence upon him."

In 1933, surrounded by Nazis and other far-right politicians, Hindenburg agreed to appoint Adolf Hitler chancellor, a position from which Hitler was able to assume dictatorial control of Germany and end the Weimar Republic. Hindenburg was allowed to remain president, though he no longer had any actual authority, until his death on August 2, 1934.

successfully ease the depression in the United States was out of the question in Germany—the inflationary crisis of the early 1920s had been the result of the reckless printing of money, and the Weimar government was so afraid of something similar reoccurring that direct infusions of money into the economy were categorically rejected.

In 1930, a desperate President Paul von Hindenburg invoked Article 48 of the Weimar constitution, which allowed the chancellor to rule by decree and bypass the Reichstag. In the face of a broken government, Hindenburg opted to go over its head. The chancellor was Heinrich Brüning, a conservative with autocratic tendencies. Brüning pursued a deflationary policy characterized by cutting government spending, slashing welfare programs, urging businesses to reduce costs however possible, and raising taxes. These policies further devastated the German citizenry, taking away the few benefits that remained to them and making their situation worse.

By the early 1930s, Weimar Germany was in desperate circumstances. The people were deeply troubled by the Great Depression, the government was too broken to do anything to address the situation, and a staunchly conservative politician was governing by decree, pursuing ineffective policies that were greatly hated by the people. The hopes of the revolution, barely over a decade in the past, had soured, as the Weimar Republic seemed incapable of living up to its promise. In this environment, a new force was able to rise to the national stage for the first time and change Germany—and the world—forever.

TELEFUNK

2

The Nazis Come to Power

The rise of the Nazis in Germany in the early 1930s was not inevitable. Though Adolf Hitler's party boasted strong organization, effective propaganda, and a message that appealed to a sizable number of people, it was the underlying problems of the Weimar government that ultimately caused the republic to fall. The Great Depression provided the immediate crisis that allowed the Nazis to gain legitimacy and have electoral success, but it was the political gridlock and lack of any real opposition, particularly from the SPD, that allowed Hitler to ascend to the chancellery on January 30, 1933. The empowerment of the elites and institutions of the right at the expense of the parties and voters of the left, which the SPD had judged necessary to maintain stability in the early days of the republic, proved

Opposite: *Adolf Hitler, leader of the Nazi Party, delivers an address a year after his appointment as German chancellor.*

to be a fatal mistake, and one that would have devastating consequences for the entire world.

Fascism and Anti-Semitism

Fascism, the political ideology most closely associated with Hitler's Nazi Party and Benito Mussolini's Fascist Party in Italy, is not a clearly defined term. Historians and political scientists to this day continue to discuss the nature of Fascism, their work complicated by the fact that the ideology is not associated with any one founding philosophical document or thinker. In addition, those texts that do exist, and which informed the ideologies of Mussolini and Hitler, were largely ignored once the Fascists and the Nazis assumed power. Fascism can manifest itself differently depending on the time and place, with individual countries pursuing Fascist ends in disparate ways. Nonetheless, some general characteristics remain constant in most instances of Fascism, and allow for at least a functional understanding of the phenomenon.

Fascism, ultimately, is a system of political and social organization that seeks to unite and rejuvenate a particular community of people whose quality of life is perceived to be in decline. This organization and rejuvenation is characterized by a belief in the superiority of the community in question, and the inferiority of other groups, an attitude expressed through aggressive nationalism and **xenophobia**, the fear and distrust of foreigners. Fascist xenophobia usually manifests itself through the scapegoating of those deemed to be outsiders, heaping blame upon them for the ills of society. Fascism is hostile to free and open democracy, instead organizing around one strong, charismatic leader. Fascists glorify war and conquest, stress the need for structure, law, and order, and hold traditional, almost romanticized, notions of loyalty, hard work, and family life. Fascism is diametrically opposed to Marxism and socialism, though it may adopt the language of or even pursue policies similar to socialism in order to unite a community.

In Germany, the core beliefs of Fascism included virulent anti-Semitism, which had a long history in Europe before the Nazi Party was even formed. The Jewish population was concentrated mostly in the East, particularly in Russia and Poland. The Jews there had been persecuted as outsiders since their first days in Europe, and that level of discrimination had continued into the nineteenth and twentieth centuries. **Pogroms** were common in Eastern Europe during this period and were often organized by the state. In Russia, Romania, and Hungary, laws had been passed that sought to limit the participation of Jews in daily life, while anti-Semitism in Poland disproportionately affected traditional Jews who were less assimilated into Polish culture. Anti-Semitism struck Western Europe as well, with the most high-profile scandal occurring in France, where a Jewish soldier was convicted of a crime there was ample evidence he did not commit.

In this environment, Germany was actually something of a haven for Jews within Europe. Many Jews fled to Germany to escape from pogroms in their native lands, and once there, they were able to assimilate into German culture.

Though anti-Semitism always existed to some degree, it was not until after World War I that it became a widespread sentiment. The myth that Germany had been "stabbed in the back" by Jews during the war spread quickly, and Jews that were clearly from another country were deemed inherently suspicious. Jews were also heavily associated with Communism which, following the Bolshevik Revolution in Russia in 1917, provided another excuse for increased hostility on the part of many Germans. In addition to these relatively new prejudices, old stereotypes about Jews controlling the business world and the media continued to be expressed, creating a toxic climate of paranoia, prejudice, and distrust. The scapegoating of Jews became an essential piece of Adolf Hitler's personal worldview, and went on to be one of the central principles of the Nazi Party.

The Ideology of Adolf Hitler

Adolf Hitler was born in Braunau-on-the-Inn, Austria, on April 20, 1889. As a boy, Hitler had a passion for history, both in school and in his reading, and from an early age he wished that all of the Germanic peoples (Austrians among them) could be united into one country. The young Hitler had a good relationship with his mother, whom he loved deeply, but often argued with his father. A retired customs official, Hitler's father wanted his son to go into government; Adolf wanted to be an artist instead, and his eventual rejection from art school would haunt him for the rest of his life.

Adolf Hitler as an infant

In 1908, Hitler's beloved mother died. Devastated, he packed a few belongings in a suitcase and set off for Vienna, to make something of his life. Hitler had no plan for what he would do at first, so he found himself wandering aimlessly, doing occasional odd jobs and living a hard, hungry life. He avoided the path of many other drifters, however, strenuously avoiding drugs and alcohol. Instead, between the works of history and philosophy that he read and the experiences he had in the city, Hitler began to develop a political ideology and an outlook on the world.

Hitler's thinking was dominated by his conception of race. Influenced by the work of previous thinkers, including Johann Herder, Arthur Schopenhauer, and Friedrich Nietzsche, Hitler came to view mankind as a series of separate races, as distinct from one another as different species of animals. He considered each race to possess (or lack) certain characteristics, and thought that the races should develop at their own paces amongst their own kind, intermingling as little as possible. The blending of races, he believed, would inevitably result in the lowering of the superior race to the level of its inferiors. These theories of racial science had grown in popularity throughout the late nineteenth century, especially after Charles Darwin's theories of natural selection had been widely disseminated. Just as "survival of the fittest" was the rule in nature, so too were some races thought to be naturally superior to others.

Influencing Hitler

Hitler also held that the German race, based on its Aryan bloodline, was the foremost race in the world. He came to this conclusion through his reading of history, particularly Oswald Spengler's wildly popular *The Decline of the West*. The book had examined history through a Social Darwinist lens, which expressed that the struggle between various races for supremacy was the true story of the past, and would continue to define the world in the future.

Spengler upheld war as "the primary politics of *everything* that lives," and articulated the idea of the Führer, an exceptional leader that would rise up and lead his people to new heights of prosperity. He even wrote about what Hitler would later articulate as National Socialism, the need for solidarity, loyalty, and sacrifice along purely racial lines, rather than the traditional socialist solidarity amongst the working classes, regardless of race or nationality.

Hitler was very influenced by Spengler's view of history, and he attributed all of the greatest advancements made by mankind to the German race, claiming that German culture was superior to all others. He desired a union of all German peoples, the *Volk*, united by their shared language, culture, and heritage, and a nation that would guarantee the ability of the race to reach its full potential. Though Hitler considered all other races to be inferior to the Germans, the one race that he singled out as being particularly noxious was the Jews.

Hitler's anti-Semitism was connected to his hatred for Marxism and socialism. He abhorred the international nature of socialism and Communism, and its push for equality amongst all people. It flew in the face of everything he had come to believe about the superiority of some races to others, and the uniquely special character of the German people. The desire of the Communists to do away with both the government of the kaiser and the concept of the German nation itself was anathema to Hitler. "The scales fell from [his] eyes;" however, when he realized that many left-wing leaders were also Jewish, this explained everything for Hitler: the reason these "agitators" were so hostile to the interests of the German race was their belonging to a different race entirely. From here, Hitler began to see Jewish influence everywhere. He believed that Jews controlled the press (using as his evidence the fact that Jewish plays often got better reviews than German plays) and were responsible for nine-tenths of the tawdry literature and theatrical productions that existed. He considered Jews incapable of creating a culture, or even existing at a level beyond mere self-preservation. Hitler eventually saw the Jew as the cause of every ill in modern society, and the largest obstacle to the German race reaching its full potential. It must also be stressed that Hitler's anti-Semitism was along racial, not religious, lines. A Jew that had converted to Christianity was still a Jew, just as a German that was living abroad was still a German. Crusading against the Jewish race on behalf of his fellow Germans became a personal mission for Hitler from this point forward.

A Place for Germans

Closely tied to Hitler's theory of race was his belief in the need for space for the German people. Once the German race was united, it needed resources and farmland in order to flourish. Hitler believed limiting the population to a fixed space with unchanging borders would lead to stagnation and eventually racial decline. Therefore, he argued for an ever-expanding populace, one that would take new lands and expel or exterminate the peoples living there—survival of the fittest on a national scale. This would require a strong military and a culture that upheld military service and sacrifice as the highest personal honor. Once new lands were conquered, the

German people would be able to expand, both geographically and numerically. The new children being born would more than make up for any casualties incurred in the taking of the territory, and when the new borders began to be constrictive, the state would expand further.

Indefinite war was therefore a measure of practical necessity for Hitler, not an option of last resort. War and conquest were required for the overall health of the race, to give it the space it needed to thrive. In Hitler's mind, this space was to be found in the East. Russia and the lands of Eastern Europe were vast and resource-rich. Moreover, the people living there were either Jews or Slavs, both races that Hitler considered deeply inferior and incapable of producing anything of value. The lands taken from them would provide the ideal ***lebensraum***, or living space, for the German nation.

These ideas of race and space developed and solidified in Hitler's mind over a period of several years in both Vienna and Munich, where he moved in 1912. When World War I broke out in 1914, Hitler greeted it with enthusiasm and willingly volunteered to fight. He viewed the war as a chance to prove his commitment to his ideals and to his nation, and as an opportunity for Germany to fight for her glorious future.

Sent home in the midst of the fighting, however, Hitler became concerned about the changes he perceived in society. He noticed that some businesses had been taken over by Jews, and that Jews were also present among the military officials who were directing operations, but not themselves at risk on the battlefield. The number of Jews in these positions was no doubt exaggerated in Hitler's mind, but the effect was an expansion of his belief that Jews were taking advantage of the war to accrue power for themselves. As the war neared its conclusion and it became apparent that Germany would be defeated, Hitler's conviction that his country had been betrayed from within was strengthened. He was devastated when the armistice was signed at the end of 1918, and regretted that so many soldiers had died in vain.

The Early Years of the Nazi Party

Following the war, Hitler found himself in a Germany he no longer recognized. He hated the republic and longed for a return to the monarchy of the kaiser. He was also incensed by the Treaty of Versailles, an act of "highway robbery" that had humiliated the German people. It was late in 1919 that an unhappy Hitler was assigned by the military to spy on a small party of the extreme right, the German Worker's Party (DAP). Finding that he agreed with the ideas expressed at the first meeting he attended, Hitler joined the party sincerely and quickly became one of its leaders and primary orators. Within a matter of months, the party had been renamed the National Socialist German Worker's Party (NSDAP), commonly referred to as the Nazi Party.

For the next three years, the Nazis agitated throughout Germany, spreading their racial ideology and holding raucous rallies. Though the party was never more than a fringe movement during this time, it nonetheless developed a structure and language that would serve it well in the years to come. Emphasis was placed on organization and discipline, and the party was structured in a top-down fashion. Party leaders made decisions, and they were followed absolutely. Committees only existed to do the work assigned to them by their superiors, not to vote on issues.

The Nazis' organization was matched by their persistence. Party members would spend extensive time in cities and villages, meeting with individual Germans and speaking in terms they could understand, often meeting with the same people day after day. Their determination was rewarded with new converts to the Nazi cause, who would in turn set off on their own into neighboring villages to spread the party message.

In addition to the internal party structure, this time period also allowed the Nazis to develop a form for their rallies. Hitler placed great emphasis on emotional, stirring oratory and propaganda as a way to unite and mobilize a base of voters. He believed that facts and data were less important than the visceral feelings of hope and inspiration; the point of propaganda and rhetoric was to convince, by any means necessary. Therefore, Nazi rallies featured fiery speeches that built to an intense climax, usually delivered by Hitler himself. Hitler made effective use of new technologies, not only microphones and loudspeakers, which enabled him to address crowds of more than a few dozen people, but also airplanes, which allowed him to make dramatic entrances to Nazi rallies, descending from the heavens as if he was a god. The message of these rallies focused on a few key tenets of the Nazi program: strong opposition to Marxism and socialism, the need for redress of the "disgrace of Versailles," the necessity of a government led by one strong leader, and anti-Semitism. Audiences were promised that Germany would expand, remilitarize, and become a world leader, and loyal followers would be rewarded with government jobs taken from their exploiters (i.e. Jews).

The Nazi flag, designed to unite its adherents under one banner, was purposely colored red to antagonize the Marxist left, who were represented by the same color. The Nazis deliberately sought to provoke a violent response from the Communists so that they could be seen as both victims of violent Marxist radicals and a force for law and order when they subdued their opponents. In this way, the entire political left (Social Democrats and Communists were lumped together as one group by the Nazis) could be painted as unruly, potentially dangerous **ideologues**. To make sure the Nazis would triumph in these clashes, the party formed its own paramilitary organization, the *Sturmabteilung* (SA), or Stormtroopers, also known as the Brown Shirts. Like other paramilitary forces, members of the SA were mostly World War I veterans with nowhere else to go, as well as enthusiastic volunteers who had converted to the Nazi cause and wanted to help the party however they could.

Nazi Party membership in the 1920s was overwhelmingly young and male, and contained many individuals who had been too young to fight in the war and felt they had missed their chance to serve their country. These men, many of them aimless and unsettled in their lives, were attracted by the sense of belonging they felt within the party. The promise of the restoration of a more traditional Germany was attractive to those who felt like strangers in the modern Weimar Republic, as was the unifying appeal of a country designed to serve the German race.

Among this generation was Joseph Goebbels, who eventually became the Nazi minister of propaganda. Born to a lower-class family and left with a clubfoot following an illness, Goebbels was short and considered himself an outsider. His family fell on hard times after the war, and Goebbels became resentful of Germany's defeat and the dire straits that followed. The Nazis presented him with an opportunity to ameliorate those grievances, and he joined in the mid-1920s, becoming essential to crafting the image of Hitler as a mythic, heroic figure that could single-handedly restore Germany to greatness.

By 1923, the Nazi Party had grown in size and had developed a firm program for administering Germany. With the inflation crisis at its peak and the Weimar government struggling to deal with it, Hitler believed that the country was ripe for a revolution. Confident the people would go along with him, he decided to attempt to overthrow the government.

Upon hearing that the state of Bavaria was considering secession in the face of Weimar's inability to control the hyperinflation, Hitler determined that the timing would never be better. A group of citizens and local leaders were gathering in the Bürgerbräukeller, a beer hall in Munich, to discuss whether or not to break with the republic. Where better to start a coup than among people who were themselves considering forming their own state?

On the night of November 8, 1923, Hitler and a group of armed Brown Shirts stormed the beer hall, where three thousand people had assembled. Firing a pistol into the air to gain attention, Hitler proclaimed, "The national revolution has begun!" He addressed the crowd, promising to form a new government with himself at the head and General Erich Ludendorff, commander of the German forces in World War I, in charge of the military. Ludendorff had not been part of the planning for the coup but came down to join Hitler once word reached him that the Nazis had taken the hall. His presence helped lend legitimacy to Hitler's proposed government, but the beer hall was a poor location from which to gain control over the city. State and local officials quickly received news of what was happening and mobilized to suppress the uprising.

On the morning of November 9, Ludendorff proposed marching into the city center and declaring it their new capital, reassuring a nervous Hitler that no one would dare attack the Nazis if a hero of the Great War was among them. He was wrong. The police opened fire on the Stormtroopers, killing sixteen Nazis and wounding many others. Hitler fled but was swiftly captured and tried, along with several other party leaders. Ludendorff alone remained unmolested; as he had predicted, his reputation was such that no officer dared

Adolf Hitler (fourth from right) *and other key figures in the Beer Hall Putsch await trial for their attempted overthrow of the government.*

fire upon him, and the justice system was unwilling to convict him for his role in the aborted coup.

As a result of the failed Beer Hall **Putsch**, the Nazis were largely discredited. The party and the SA were both temporarily banned (though neither ever fully ceased to exist), and the leaders of the movement were arrested and tried for treason. Despite acting as his own defense and making passionate speeches in the courtroom, Hitler was sentenced to five years in Landsberg prison. While there, Hitler took stock of his situation and used the time to write a book. His sentence was commuted within less than a year, and by the end of 1924, Hitler was a free man. His next step was to publish what he had written.

The Nazis Regroup and the Opposition Falters

Mein Kampf (*My Struggle*) was part autobiography and part manifesto. Hitler outlined the details of his life and the circumstances surrounding the birth of the Nazi Party, in addition to fully articulating his political and social worldview. Published in two volumes, the work described the problems of democracy and the dangers posed by Marxists and Jews. Hitler made clear that he thought democracy was simply a step along the path to Communism, and that a parliamentary system like the one that currently existed in Germany would inevitably be obstructed by disagreements among its members, who never bore any responsibility or faced any real consequences for their decisions. Hitler emphasized the need for one leader, chosen by the people, to make decisions and rule the country.

Mein Kampf also explored Hitler's theories of race, particularly his hatred for Jews. Hitler described the Jews in truly disgusting terms, comparing them to bacteria, maggots, and parasites, with the goal of rendering them subhuman in the eyes of his readers. By doing so, Hitler created a common enemy, one that was responsible for everything wrong with modern society, and a force that the German people could rally against. This philosophy, combined with the book's glorification of the Aryan race and call for its aggressive expansion into the East, provided the blueprint for everything that the Nazis would do once they acquired power.

Hitler's program as outlined in *Mein Kampf* also acted as the driving force behind Nazi rallies going forward.

Adolf Hitler speaks to a crowd at a Nazi rally in 1933.

Having learned the lesson of the failed putsch attempt, Hitler determined that the Nazis would now work entirely within the system. An armed revolt could be crushed, but a party that was legally elected could not be prevented from coming to power. Throughout the mid-1920s, the Nazis continued to agitate and hold rallies much like those they had held earlier in the decade. The messaging became smoother and more unified around Hitler's central tenets of anti-Semitism, anti-Marxism, and extreme nationalism, and the staging of rallies became increasingly well organized and spectacular. By the end of the decade, Adolf Hitler and the Nazis had successfully articulated a clear vision of what Germany's future could look like, enumerated a series of goals to make that future a reality, and developed an apparatus capable of spreading their message across the country. This clarity of purpose, unity of vision, and organizational rigor would prove decisive in the crisis brought about by the Great Depression.

The depression had left Germany in a precarious position. In 1930, unemployment was rising, the government was at a standstill, and Chancellor Heinrich Brüning was ruling by decree. His austerity measures were failing to offer any relief from the economic catastrophe. Instead, they angered the population and increased their disillusionment with the shape of the republic. Into this environment came the Nazis, railing against the government that had failed to help its people and blaming one specific enemy for the worldwide economic downturn. Brüning foolishly called for elections in the fall of 1930, confident that his party would win a majority of seats, allowing him to govern with even less opposition. Instead, the Nazis won 18.3 percent of the vote, giving them 107 seats in the Reichstag. Once a fringe group, the NSDAP was now a major political party.

The elections did not alter the circumstances within the Reichstag in any meaningful way—the government was still just as gridlocked as before. However, this did not deter the Nazis. They continued to agitate and propagandize as they had been doing for several years, only now with a much higher platform. Support for the Nazis increased as the depression continued to grind on and their message was spread. Adolf Hitler's moment had arrived, and his party took full advantage of the crisis of German democracy.

The SPD, the party most responsible for the construction of the Weimar Republic and its staunchest defender, was left rudderless. The Social Democrats had no answer for the Great Depression, the unemployment insurance program they had championed having gone bankrupt only a few months into the crisis. Unable to articulate a coherent alternative plan, the party began to bleed support. Those arguing for direct relief to the workers and others hardest hit by the depression went to the left, inflating the membership of the KPD. Others went to the right, seeking a more authoritarian solution. Sadly, it was the ineffective SPD, more than any other party in Weimar Germany, that took the Nazi threat seriously.

Attempts by the SPD (and other, smaller parties) to stop the Nazis during 1931 and 1932 consisted of "toleration," the willingness to accept the policies and politicians of the far right in the short term in the hopes of preserving the republic in the long term. In practice, this meant that the SPD offered little resistance to Brüning's government or his deflationary policies. It also meant that in the presidential election of 1932, the SPD supported Paul von Hindenburg, the incumbent president and war hero who had initially won office with the support of the right. His opponent was Adolf Hitler himself, so the choice of the SPD to support the "lesser evil" is entirely understandable, but the overall impression of the SPD among its supporters continued to sour.

Though Hindenburg won the election, he was now in his eighties and remained a symbol of the old imperial regime. The SPD, ostensibly to protect democracy, was embracing plainly anti-democratic politicians in Hindenburg and Brüning. The party had become impervious to the demands of its members, and its call for preservation of the government increasingly fell on deaf ears. The party failed to recognize that a government utterly incapable of meeting the basic needs of its starving, out-of-work population is not a government worth preserving.

The KPD did offer a remedy for the economic calamity. The Great Depression was seen as the final crisis of capitalism, a fulfillment of what Karl Marx had written nearly a century earlier, and the KPD believed that the time had come for the establishment of a Communist system of government. This widened the split that already existed between the Communists and the SPD, a split that stretched back to the earliest days of the republic. The KPD had not forgotten that its founders had been executed by paramilitaries working for the SPD, nor that the Social Democrats had chosen the interests of the elite, capitalist right over the interests of the striking, labor left. Now, when the SPD most needed help, the KPD refused to give it. The Social Democrats were tolerating the Brüning government as it dismantled the social welfare system, all in a desperate bid to maintain the existing governmental structure. This ran directly counter to the program of the Communists, and resulted in their labeling the SPD "social Fascists."

Changes

On May 30, 1932, Brüning was removed from his position as chancellor by President Hindenburg. Brüning's budget-cutting mania was now threatening the subsidies of wealthy Prussian estate owners, a sacrifice that the elites were not willing to make. The new chancellor, Franz von Papen, was an authoritarian with ambitions of ending the republic. He installed his own government in the state of Prussia, throwing out the elected, mostly SPD representatives, and calling for a new round of elections throughout the country.

Like Brüning, Papen felt confident that the people would overwhelmingly support his agenda. Like Brüning, he was wrong. Papen had done nothing to alleviate the crushing weight of the depression, and so the elections of July 31 resulted in the Nazis receiving 37.3 percent support. Having won more votes than any other party, the Nazis now held 230 seats in the Reichstag and quickly motioned for a vote of no confidence in the chancellor. The KPD supported this motion, which removed Papen from the chancellery and triggered yet another round of elections.

In the November 1932 balloting, the Nazis fell to 33.1 percent of the vote, reducing the number of seats they held to 196. In addition to this regression, Hindenburg denied Hitler's request to be made chancellor, instead appointing Kurt von Schleicher. While Schleicher attempted to pursue a jobs program, the Nazis began negotiations to ensure their power did not continue to erode.

The Fall of the Weimar Republic

Meeting with the parties and interests of the established right (the DNVP, military officials, business elites, and old nobility), the Nazis sought a compromise that would allow

THE VOTING BASE OF THE NAZI PARTY

The voting base of the Nazi Party represented a wide array of German citizens. Middle and lower-middle class professionals and small business owners were most likely to support the Nazis since they felt economically and socially insecure. This group included shopkeepers, artisans, lawyers, and domestic servants. These voters were not those who had suffered most from the depression, but rather those whose financial and social positions had been made newly precarious. Though not unemployed yet, they were in danger of being so, as their profits had decreased and their businesses had stagnated. Increasing modernization was also a fear for many small shopkeepers, who worried they would be rendered irrelevant. This voting bloc was dissatisfied with the current government and desired a return to a previous state of financial security and perceived class status. In the Nazis, these voters felt they had found a party that could help them protect what they had and regain what they had lost.

Nazi voters were also largely rural. The Germans that lived outside of the big cities tended to be more hostile to the republic in general, even before the Nazis began courting their votes. These rural voters were mostly middle and lower-middle class, like their more urban counterparts, and tended to be younger (twenty-one to forty years old). They were also socially conservative and distrustful of government bureaucracy, both key elements of the Nazi program.

them to take power. Both the Nazis and the other members of the right were after self-advancement in these meetings and looked on their negotiating partner as a means to that end.

The military, bureaucratic, and business elites of the right had been hostile to the Weimar Republic from its inception, and had spent the last decade trying to bring about a more authoritarian regime. Many of these elites had lived a better life under the kaiser, wielding more power and influence over the government. Now they wished for a return to those conditions. Business and industrial leaders wanted to operate without regulation, the military wanted to see Germany restored to her former glory, and almost all members of the right wanted to see greater restrictions placed on Jews, socialists, and the modern social values that had come to Germany. The previous hesitation of the right to ally with the Nazis was not due to major ideological differences but rather the volatile and, more importantly, uncontrollable nature of the NSDAP.

By early 1933, the established right was willing to take a chance. All their other efforts to take power had failed, and with the Nazis' share of the vote diminishing (and support for the Communists on the rise), it seemed like the window of opportunity brought about by the depression was closing.

For their part, the Nazis needed a wider base of support from the political and economic establishment. The loss of seats in the November elections had shaken the party and raised concerns that a broader coalition was necessary to give the Nazis enough power to fully implement their agenda. This

Adolf Hitler with the man who appointed him chancellor, President Paul von Hindenburg.

coalition was never binding, in Hitler's mind. Indeed, he had written in *Mein Kampf* that treaties and agreements are made to be broken and that as soon as a pact ceases to be beneficial to the Volk, it should be dissolved. The agreement that was ultimately reached called for Hitler to serve as chancellor, with Franz von Papen as his vice-chancellor. Of the other ten members of the government appointed by Hindenburg, only two would be members of the Nazi Party. This arrangement inspired confidence among the conservative elites, who believed that they would be able to control the direction of the new government. They were wrong.

Adolf Hitler was appointed chancellor of Germany on January 30, 1933. Within months, the Weimar Republic was dead, and Hitler was leading a Fascist dictatorship.

The horrors perpetrated by that dictatorship would define the twentieth century and completely change the course of history.

A number of factors brought Hitler to power, not least among them the Great Depression, which produced a crisis that paralyzed the government and allowed a Fascist demagogue to offer a seductive solution that scapegoated a vulnerable minority population. The Treaty of Versailles also contributed to Hitler's rise, as its harsh punishments both humiliated the German people and initially had devastating effects on its economy. The desire for a politician to redress the grievances brought about by the Treaty of Versailles and restore Germany to its former status was widespread and powerful. More important than the depression or the treaty, however, was the underlying fragility and instability of the Weimar Republic. The fracturing of interests at the start of the republic proved fatal during its last years, as the pathologies of the left, right, and center combined to bring Hitler to power.

The SPD violently suppressing the Communist left in early 1919 marked the beginning of a bitter, deeply hostile split that eventually had dire consequences. The Social Democrats had initially thought it necessary to turn their backs on the far left for the good of the republic. In the end, this prevented the formation of a coalition that might have been able to counter the Nazis. The SPD's instincts toward moderation and eventually toleration deepened the hatred of the KPD for the Social Democrats, dooming any chance of

TIMELINE OF HITLER'S RISE TO POWER

1919 Hitler joins what will later become the Nazi Party.

1923 Hitler fails to overthrow the government and is arrested.

1924 Hitler serves time in prison and begins writing *Mein Kampf*.

1925 The first volume of *Mein Kampf* is published.

1929 The Great Depression begins.

1930 The Reichstag descends into gridlock and Heinrich Brüning begins ruling by decree; the Nazis win significant representation in the Reichstag.

1932 Hindenburg reelected president; the Nazis become the largest party in the Reichstag and remove the chancellor; Hindenburg denies Hitler the chancellery; the Nazis lose seats at the end of the year.

1933 The Nazis begin negotiating with the politicians and other leaders of the right; a deal is struck, and Hitler is appointed chancellor on January 30.

building an effective opposition. The parties and institutions of the right, hostile to the republic and the very concept of democracy from the beginning, were also crucial in the ascent of Hitler. It was these interests, after all, which appointed him to the chancellery.

In a broader context, however, the failure to strip the old imperial elite of its power following World War I proved to be another colossal blunder in the early months of Weimar. By allowing military and bureaucratic officials, industrial leaders, judges, and influential members of the clergy to maintain their authority, wealth, and status, the Weimar coalition guaranteed that a well-funded, well-connected, largely anti-democratic right would exist to oppose the new republic at every turn. The hostility of the right to democracy, as well as its increasing embrace of anti-Semitism and repetition of the myth that Germany had been "stabbed in the back" and betrayed by the Treaty of Versailles, made for a noxious climate in Germany, one that the Nazis eagerly embraced and exploited. In the end, it was the unbroken power of these elite, right-wing institutions that gave them the ability to negotiate with Hitler and eventually bring him to power. This outcome was not inevitable; had the other parties in Germany reacted differently to Hitler's rise, his ultimate triumph could have been prevented. Unfortunately, the schisms within the republic were too deep to be overcome.

Rheingold
Kaiser Saal
TANZ-ABEND
5 Uhr
DOPPEL-KONZERT
AQUARIUM
B. T. L.
35000 M.
Lose
zu M 3.60

3

Cultural and Social Changes in Weimar Germany

During its short life, Weimar Germany developed a distinctly modern society and a rich culture. Changing social mores led to a relaxation of gender norms, particularly for women, and new technologies both changed daily life and benefited the arts. This societal openness and artistic freedom was revolutionary, but also tragically brief. The positive social reforms of the Weimar Republic were rolled back by the Nazis, and the arts were repurposed to serve the interests of the state. This caused a mass exodus of artists to the West, many of them landing in the United States, where they were joined by scientists and academics that had been forced out of Germany for their Jewish heritage. The departure of so many influential artists and intellectuals, whether voluntary or not, brought the cultural flowering of Weimar to an abrupt end.

Opposite: *Berlin in the 1920s was a bustling, thoroughly modern metropolis.*

The New Weimar Culture

The cultural renaissance of Germany in the 1920s was centered in Berlin. With four million residents, Berlin was the second-largest city in Europe and the most plainly modern city in the Weimar Republic. All of the newest technologies and luxuries could be found there. Jazz, the newest American form of music, emanated from the city's nightclubs. The presence of Jews, foreign travelers, and immigrants was apparent. Women and other traditionally marginalized individuals, such as homosexual and transgendered people, lived freely in the city and sexual mores became less restrictive.

This opening of Weimar society, coinciding with the opening of German political life during and after the revolution, also breathed new life into the arts. Painters, writers, poets, filmmakers, and architects were able to meet with one another and draw inspiration from the big city. As a result, they produced some of the most important cultural artifacts of this period within its borders.

Berlin's modernity was a subject of criticism for some conservative Germans, who disdained the city for its internationalism and its perceived loose moral character; this critique was later picked up by the Nazis. While the republic lasted, however, Berlin was emblematic of its culture as a whole: new, exciting, and looking with hope to the future.

One of the most obvious examples of this modern culture was "the New Woman." Like the flappers of America in the 1920s, the New Woman in Germany was identifiable by her short hair, generally thin figure, unique style of dress, and disdain for traditional gender roles. She did as she pleased, refusing to cater to the old notions of what a woman "should" spend her time doing. The New Woman smoked, occasionally wore men's clothing, and kept company with whomever she chose. While this particular type of New Woman remained a largely upper- and middle-class phenomenon, women from all parts of Weimar Germany became a more visible presence during this era. They had received the right to vote under the new republic, and new employment opportunities were opened up to them after the war. Department stores often hired young women to help drive foot traffic and assist customers with their shopping, and an increased need for white-collar workers allowed urban women to live a relatively comfortable middle-class lifestyle. While this by no means represented full gender equality, it was still an important break from the conservative, prewar values that had kept women in mostly maternal roles.

The Impact of Modern Technology

Weimar Germany ushered in a boom in new technologies and the democratization of old ones. Sound amplification devices saw their first widespread distribution, as microphones and loudspeakers made public speaking easier than ever before, and the phonograph revolutionized the way music was consumed. Recorded music could now be played loudly and clearly in both private homes and in businesses, an innovation that offered customers a more refined shopping experience.

The culmination of the advancement in sound technology was the radio. By 1932, a quarter of all German households owned a radio, and more people listened to the radio than went to the cinema. Artists had to adapt to the new medium, rewriting plays to make them fully coherent in audio form and honing musical performances to make them utterly flawless; a missed note was much more noticeable over the radio than in a concert hall. The radio was a potent new tool for mass communication, allowing millions of Germans to receive a message simultaneously. As a result, the government took a great deal of interest in what messages were being delivered. Government involvement with the radio was initially limited to licensing what was broadcast, but by 1932, the government had assumed full control of the industry.

Photography was made more available to the average citizen during the Weimar period, and as a result, it was also caught up in the conversation regarding mass messaging. On the individual level, cameras became affordable to the ordinary German for the first time in the 1920s, and in 1925 Leica introduced a small, easily portable camera with high image quality. This turned photography into an amateur hobby as well as a professional field of art. August Sander and László Moholy-Nagy became famous for their photographs, and Hannah Höch broke ground with her work in photomontage.

Ads in newspapers and magazines used photos in addition to traditional illustrations to better sell a lifestyle to readers. Images of young, fresh-faced, beautiful people set new (and often unrealistic) standards for what the human body should look like, and photographs of exotic foreign locales allowed German citizens to glimpse parts of the world they had only been able to imagine before. The power of these advertisements, in both stimulating commerce and creating an ideal physical appearance toward which young men and women strived, demonstrated the power of photography on a mass level.

Film

Film in the Weimar Republic was a medium that combined artistry and widespread distribution in a way that was matched only by radio. It was democratic and accessible to Germans across all class lines in a way that opera, the theater, and even cheap novels were not. The cinema acted as escapism, entertainment, and art all at once, and it provides a solid case study for both the changing artistic movements within Weimar as well as the impact of the Nazi takeover on both artists and their medium.

In the first days of the Weimar Republic, film was largely seen as a distraction and a form of entertainment for the lower classes. Passionate filmmakers soon began to elevate the quality of German cinema, however, turning it into a modern art form that would go on to be exhibited in massive, ornately designed theaters. The dominant artistic movement during the first half of the Weimar Republic was **Expressionism,** which sought to probe the psychological depths of individuals and societies and represent interior

FRITZ LANG: THE FILMMAKER THAT FLED

An Expressionist vision of the future, as realized by Fritz Lang in Metropolis

Fritz Lang was one of the most celebrated artists in Weimar Germany. Born in Vienna in 1890, Lang rose to prominence with *Der müde Tod* (*Destiny*, 1921), an expansive fantasy that dealt with the inevitability of death, a common theme in postwar German art. Lang, who had trained as an architect, had been consulted during the production of *The Cabinet of Dr. Caligari*, and his films became known for their geometric stylization and striking lighting. Lang's Expressionist masterpiece was *Metropolis* (1927), which told the story of a futuristic totalitarian city where men served machines. The film boasted innovative special effects and a unique visual look, featuring images that would go on to inspire the design of such films as *Star Wars* (1977) and *Blade Runner* (1982).

Many actors and directors struggled to adjust to the introduction of sound into motion pictures in the late 1920s, but Lang quickly mastered the new technology. *M* (1931), starring Peter Lorre, used sound cinematically, particularly in the chilling whistle of the film's antagonist. *M* cemented Lang's reputation as one of the foremost filmmakers in Germany, and it was partially for this reason that he was approached by Hitler and Minister of Propaganda Joseph Goebbels following the Nazi takeover. *Metropolis* was Hitler's favorite film, and the Führer wanted Lang to take over the German film industry. Lang, a political liberal and half-Jewish himself, refused the offer, unwilling to collaborate with the Nazis. Gathering some belongings, he fled the country.

Lang first settled in Paris, and shortly after came to Hollywood. There, his career continued for another two decades. Like other German émigré filmmakers, Lang brought the artistic techniques of Expressionism to American films, influencing their lighting, set design, and overall aesthetic. His most well-known American productions were *films noir*, dark, gritty movies that featured sordid characters, unique stylizations, and explored many of the same themes as German Expressionism. Lang died in 1976, and is today remembered as one of the most talented and influential filmmakers to emerge from Germany in the first half of the twentieth century.

A poster for The Cabinet of Dr. Caligari. *Note the sharp angles and exaggerated stylizations, both hallmarks of German Expressionism.*

feelings through exterior mediums. Often preoccupied with violence and disorientation, German Expressionism grew out of the dislocation and psychological scars of World War I, and attempted to reckon with a world in which such destruction was possible. This movement influenced filmmakers like Robert Wiene with his film *The Cabinet of Dr. Caligari* (1920), F. W. Murnau and *Nosferatu* (1922) and Fritz Lang and *Metropolis* (1927). The editing, camerawork, and lighting of these German Expressionist films would go on to be a major influence on the imagery and visual style of most horror films of the early 1930s in the United States.

In the mid-1920s, realism began to make a comeback in the arts, with a move away from overt stylization toward moderation and accurate representation of daily life. Murnau's *The Last Laugh* (1924) was a more restrained, realistic film, albeit one that still maintained the psychological exploration of his earlier Expressionist works. *Berlin: Symphony of a City* (1927), directed by Walter Ruttmann, was pure realism, and took a documentary look at a day in the life of the city of Berlin.

At the same time that German films were shifting in their style, American films began pouring into the country. Following the Dawes Plan and the economic stabilization in 1924, American production studios began sending their films to Germany, where they proved incredibly popular. While German filmmakers were pushing artistic boundaries and providing visual representation for complex psychological realities, audiences flocked to Charlie Chaplin comedies and basic melodramas. This preference for foreign imports began to have a negative financial impact on the German film industry, and German filmmakers and actors (including Murnau) began immigrating to the United States.

The German film industry was therefore in decline when the Nazis came to power, its financial difficulties and loss of talent beginning to impact the quality of pictures produced. Joseph Goebbels, in charge of the German film industry from 1933 onwards, made the best of the artists that remained to him. "Degenerate art" was banned under the Nazis, and the Reich Cinema Law of 1934 prevented Jews from working in the industry. The more artistic side of the cinema was stripped out, both by Nazi content controls as well as the dearth of talented filmmakers.

Departures of Germany's most gifted cinematic artists increased exponentially once the Nazis came to power, with directors and actors including Fritz Lang, Billy Wilder, Fred Zinnemann, Marlene Dietrich, and Peter Lorre all leaving the country. These political refugees went on to make long-lasting contributions to American cinema, directing and starring in some of the most influential films of the next three decades. German contributions to world cinema, by contrast, ground to a halt. Despite this, the film industry was actually one of the *least* altered of the artistic fields under the Nazis. Both Goebbels and Hitler were fans of movies and wanted to maintain as much continuity in the industry as possible. Though Hitler and Goebbels recognized the power of film for reaching mass audiences, they also believed that overt propaganda would be unpopular with German moviegoers and would therefore be ineffective. The result was a film industry that produced mostly light entertainment and escapist fiction. In all, less than a quarter of the films produced under the Nazis could be categorized as blatant propaganda.

Changes to the Arts and Sciences Under the Nazis

"Just as a Christian age could have only a Christian art," Hitler had remarked, "so a National Socialist age could have only a National Socialist art." The Nazi approach to the arts was to reshape them along racial and nationalist lines, ensuring that the themes and issues that were explored upheld Hitler's worldview. In practice, this meant the blacklisting of thousands of artists deemed subversive and a mass emigration of talent from Germany to the West. August Sander, who photographed Germans of all types, not just the Nazi ideal, had his work banned. His contemporary, the more Expressionistic László Moholy-Nagy, fled the country. An estimated 2,500 writers also left Germany, either voluntarily or under duress. Among them were the novelists Thomas Mann and Erich Maria Remarque (author of *All Quiet on the Western Front*), as well as prominent thinkers including Hans Morgenthau, Theodor Adorno, and Herbert Marcuse.

Weimar theater was also overhauled once the Nazis took power. The most popular production of the 1920s was *The Threepenny Opera*, written by Bertolt Brecht and with music by Kurt Weill. The opera was thoroughly modern, with new music that incorporated elements of jazz, contemporary slang

LENI RIEFENSTAHL: THE FILMMAKER THAT STAYED

Leni Riefenstahl became the unofficial Nazi documentarian, making films that glorified Hitler and his regime. The decision to work with the Nazis haunted Riefenstahl for the rest of her life, and justifiably overshadowed the rest of her career.

Born in the industrial town of Wedding on August 22, 1902, Riefenstahl wanted to be a dancer and an actress. She studied dance against her father's wishes, but following an injury, she transitioned to the world of film, first as an actress and then as a director. Hitler was a great admirer of Riefenstahl's work, describing a scene in which she danced on screen as "the most beautiful thing I have ever seen in a film." Her first directorial effort, *The Blue Light* (1932), also impressed him.

For her part, Riefenstahl had been captivated by Hitler during a Nazi rally in 1932, describing the experience as akin to "being struck by lightning." She wrote to him soon after, and a meeting between the two was arranged. Hitler was enamored of her, and saw in her an example of the Nazi ideal woman. He suggested that she make movies for him if he ever came to power, and after some initial misgivings, she agreed.

The two most notable films of the Nazi period were both "documentaries" personally commissioned by Adolf Hitler and directed by Leni Riefenstahl. Her first project, *Triumph of the Will* (1935), captured a Nazi rally in the city of Nuremberg, and depicted it as an almost mythic event. Hitler was presented as a godlike figure, giving impassioned speeches to groups of loyal supporters so vast they stretched beyond the horizon. Riefenstahl's second film for Hitler was *Olympia* (1938), a record of the 1936 Olympic Games in Munich. Hitler had wanted to impress the world with the success

Leni Riefenstahl attended a Nazi rally in 1934 as part of the filming of Triumph of the Will.

and power of Germany at the Games, and *Olympia* was meant to offer visual proof. The film stood as a monument to the might of Hitler's Germany, and the physical prowess that he believed gave the country its strength. Both films have since gone down in cinema history as landmark examples of propaganda.

Riefenstahl's association with the Nazis, and in particular her close relationship with Hitler himself, was a shadow from which she was unable to escape. Though she never formally joined the Nazi Party and attempted to distance herself from Hitler once World War II began, the stain of her earlier collaboration proved impossible to remove, and her film career never recovered. Riefenstahl died in 2003, at the age of 101.

terminology, and a storyline that criticized capitalism, war, and prudish sexual morality. Audiences loved it, and the popularity of the opera led to multiple foreign adaptations. American versions of the production were particularly successful, and the song "Mack the Knife," adapted from a piece in the German original, became a massive commercial hit for Bobby Darin in the 1950s.

Brecht and Weill were among those exiled from Nazi Germany, eventually settling in the United States. The theater scene they left behind was stripped of anything modern, and virtually all of the shows that were staged were old German classics that demonstrated the rich cultural heritage of the German race. Plays and operas containing elements that contradicted the tenets of Nazi ideology were suppressed, and Jewish directors, playwrights, and actors were banned. The freshness and excitement that had been injected into the theater by *The Threepenny Opera* was gone, with productions becoming safe, boring, and irrelevant.

The exodus of academic and cultural talents from Nazi Germany was not limited to the fine arts, but included the sciences as well. Germany had a rich scientific tradition before Hitler came to power, one which included Wilhelm Röntgen (who discovered X-rays), Max Planck (the founder of quantum theory), Werner Heisenberg, and Albert Einstein. German science was so far advanced that, in the first two decades of the twentieth century, more than half of the Nobel Prizes awarded in medicine and the sciences went to German nationals. Many German scientists were also Jewish. This became an issue when, on April 7, 1933, the Nazis passed a law dismissing Jews and other non-Aryans from the civil service. Since many German scientists worked at state-run universities, they found themselves suddenly out of a job. Dismissals were abrupt and arbitrary, with many of those affected fired in the midst of their research. In all, some 2,600 scientists and other scholars left Germany within the first year of the new law, a devastating setback for German science. Friends and colleagues were often unwilling to speak out on behalf of those dismissed, afraid that they would be the next to lose their situation and be targeted. One of the brave few who did attempt to intercede was Max Planck. He pleaded with Hitler not to dismiss the Jewish chemist Fritz Haber, to which Hitler responded, "If science cannot do without Jews, then we will have to do without science for a few years."

The most prominent scientist affected by the German crackdown on Jews was Albert Einstein. Already world famous long before the Nazis came to power, Einstein's theories of relativity had been proposed in 1905 and 1917, and he had won the Nobel Prize in 1921. He was also well known for his pacifism and internationalism. Einstein was in the United States when Hitler came to power, so he was not personally disrupted by the dismissal of Jews from the civil service, but he nevertheless condemned the law and Hitler's government as a whole. He renounced his German citizenship and also voluntarily resigned his position with the Prussian Academy of Sciences. Einstein's statements and actions held tremendous symbolic value. He was the most high-profile German to utterly reject the Nazis, doing so in such a direct way that it embarrassed the new regime. Having a respected, influential, well-known German condemn the party and publicly register his disgust with its actions served to damage the credibility of the Nazis in a way that statements of disapproval from other world leaders did not. It was clearly personal for Einstein, and the juxtaposition of the peaceful

Albert Einstein was the most prominent scientist to take a public stand against Adolf Hitler's Nazi regime.

man of science with the aggressive, hateful Nazi Party made clear the character of the new Germany. The practical impact of Einstein's statement may have been slight, but it was an important, courageous stand to take, and one that helped shape world opinion toward the Nazis in the first days of their power.

Less than a year after the Nazi takeover, the last vestiges of Weimar cultural and societal progress had been eliminated. Artists were blacklisted for their subversive work, and Jewish scientists and academics were removed from their posts. Thousands fled the country, leaving behind a massive artistic and intellectual vacuum. The progressive social values of Weimar were reversed by the Nazis, who certainly did not believe in the equality of all people and imposed rigid gender norms. Indeed, in all aspects of life, the Nazis rolled back the progress that had been made by the Weimar Republic.

While it lasted, however, the culture and society of Weimar managed to have substantial influence. Its legacy can still be seen in film and in theater, in music and in literature. Though overshadowed by the calamitous events that followed the fall of the republic, the story of Weimar's lost culture is its own tragedy: a flowering of artistic thought and social progress, which promised to open new areas of expression and acceptance, abruptly halted by the rise of a dark, hateful ideology.

Upon Adolf Hitler's appointment as German chancellor, the Nazis immediately began taking steps to implement their agenda. In the short term, the NSDAP sought to consolidate its power by establishing a Fascist dictatorship and reordering German life according to the party line. In the longer term, Hitler started to enact policies that would allow him to realize his goals of racial purification and territorial expansion. These programs, characterized by rabid anti-Semitism and renewed militarism, were the first steps along the road that terminated in the Holocaust and World War II.

The Formation of the Third Reich

The Nazi consolidation of power first required the neutering of Germany's rival political parties. Always willing to take

Opposite: *Becoming chancellor in 1933, Adolf Hitler quickly took steps to secure his power and assume dictatorial control of Germany.*

advantage of fortuitous circumstances, Hitler seized an opportunity presented to him at the end of his first month in office. On the night of February 27, 1933, a fire started at the Reichstag building. The culprit was a Dutch Communist who had hoped to spur a wave of anti-Fascist action; precisely the opposite ensued. German Communists were blamed as his co-conspirators, and Hitler expanded the net of blame to include the Social Democrats. Under the guise of maintaining law and order, the Nazis cracked down on socialists, Communists, labor leaders, and any other prominent leftists that could be found. The SPD press and other socialist newspapers were banned, restrictions were placed on the freedom of speech, and hundreds of left-wing party functionaries were arrested. The socialists and Communists that were detained in these early days of the Nazi regime became the first inmates of the concentration camps.

The aftermath of the Reichstag fire, which led to the suppression of the political left in Hitler's Germany

The elimination of rival parties was quickly accomplished following the Reichstag fire. Hitler had already called for new elections and, with the KPD and SPD now being actively suppressed by the state, the Nazis won 43.9 percent of the vote on March 5. Together with the DNVP, the Nazis held a majority coalition in the Reichstag and swiftly passed the Enabling Act. This allowed Hitler to pass laws without the consent of the Reichstag, effectively making him a dictator. The SPD offices were occupied by the Nazis on May 10, and party officials were beaten and harassed. The parties of the right and center were also attacked, with the Nazis unwilling to brook any rivals. By the middle of July 1933, all political parties other than the Nazis had been dissolved.

With the potential for political challenges foreclosed on, Hitler next turned his attention to securing the loyalty of the German military. The military was the only group in the country that had the ability to forcibly remove Hitler from power, making their acquiescence to the new regime an issue of paramount importance. In addition to this immediate practical concern, Hitler also knew that he needed the military if he was to achieve any of his larger goals. Beyond the obvious necessity of a strong military to conquer the lands to the east he so desperately craved, Hitler's plans for economic recovery also relied on the army. Hitler therefore began meeting with the top military officials in the country shortly after coming to power.

The burgeoning relationship between Hitler and the army was threatened, however, by an unexpected foe. The leadership of the Nazi Stormtroopers, personified by Ernst Röhm, was growing restless. Röhm and his allies, both within the SA and within the Nazi Party at large, wanted a "second revolution," a social transformation that would include integrating the SA with the German army. This would, in effect, put the leaders of the Brown Shirts at the head of the German military, a change that Hitler knew he could not let come to pass. As far back as *Mein Kampf*, Hitler had articulated the limitations of the SA—while it was an effective force for street-level politics and agitation, it was too disorganized and its leaders too undisciplined to ever be an effective, large-scale military organization. With the Nazis now safely in power, the SA had become largely unnecessary.

In 1934, tensions between Hitler, the military, and the SA came to a head. Röhm and his cohorts were becoming increasingly hostile to Hitler and the Nazi Party leadership, while military officials made it clear that they wanted to get rid of the paramilitary organization entirely. At the same time, President Paul von Hindenburg was in failing health, and his death seemed imminent. Once again seizing an opportunity, Hitler struck a deal. Knowing that he needed the existing military and its current, experienced corps of officers, Hitler agreed to suppress the SA and rebuild the German army, as long as the generals supported his installation as president following the death of Hindenburg. The generals agreed to these terms, and Hitler quickly set about fulfilling his end of the bargain.

On June 30, 1934, the Nazi Blood Purge (also known as the Night of Long Knives) took place. Over the course of the night, leaders of the SA—and any other figures that Hitler considered enemies—were summarily executed, ridding the Nazi Party of its last challengers to Hitler's leadership. In all, around one thousand people were killed in the Purge, with Hitler settling many personal scores (he oversaw the arrest and execution of Röhm himself, for one). A few days later, Hitler gave a speech in the Reichstag in which he took full responsibility for the murders. Claiming that those killed were part of a conspiracy to overthrow him, Hitler argued that he had had no choice but to act. Soon after, on August 2, President Hindenburg died, and Hitler assumed the office of the presidency, in addition to his position as chancellor.

With the Blood Purge and Hindenburg's death, Hitler's consolidation of power was complete. He now ruled with utter surety, with no institutional or military check to his power. The German army was loyal to the Führer, and meetings of the Reichstag were rarely held. Elections took the form of **plebiscites**, referendums on specific issues that offered the public little actual choice. The SA was essentially destroyed, its place taken by the *Schutzstaffel*, or SS. Originally formed as a branch of the SA, the SS had initially served as a kind of personal bodyguard to Hitler and other top Nazi officials; it now became the primary paramilitary wing of the Nazi Party. During World War II, the SS formed special military detachments and was primarily responsible for running the Nazi concentration camps and carrying out the Holocaust.

Within Germany, the SS established the Gestapo, the secret police force that used terror to keep control of the country. Operating under the principle that individual liberties and due process were less important than public security, the Gestapo was given legal impunity by the Nazis to maintain order by any means necessary. With the army, police, and government under his total control, Hitler's power was secure, and a new German Empire—the Third Reich—was firmly established.

Rearmament of the military proceeded with vigor following the Blood Purge in 1934, providing jobs and stimulating the economy. Germany's road system was revolutionized under the Nazis, largely so that military equipment and personnel could be transported more effectively across the country. Shipyards were prepared for the construction of naval vessels that could rival those of Great Britain, and a massive synthetic oil industry was created, primarily for use in fueling military vehicles. These projects helped Germany emerge from the Great Depression. Employment went up, the cost of living for the average German remained low, and travel and certain luxury items were cheap. Despite the curtailments of civil liberties, overall morale in Germany remained high.

Other cultural and political institutions were also restructured by the Nazis. Education was overhauled, with curriculums made to adhere to party ideology. History was now taught in the way that Hitler conceived of it, as a clashing of distinct races in which the Germans always triumphed. Education was also dedicated to stimulating national pride and developing a sense of idealism for the glorious future of the German people. Stress was placed on physical activity, as Hitler wanted a nation of healthy, vigorous young men that could help their Fatherland in battle. The Christian churches were suppressed under the Nazis, as they provided systems of authority and structure that were wholly separate from the state. Religion was recast around almost pagan lines, with Jesus reimagined as a Germanic war hero to undercut the power of both Catholic and Protestant tradition at every possible opportunity. Other Nazi policies were aimed at enhancing conformity and imparting party ideology from an early age. The Hitler Youth, a program for German teenagers, operated as an arm of the Nazi Party, indoctrinating young people with Nazi propaganda and encouraging their loyalty to the state. Clothing guidelines were established to offer a visual definition for what it meant to be of the German race, and Jews were prevented from purchasing certain items.

Anti-Semitic Persecution and the Holocaust

The anti-Semitism that had characterized Hitler's personal philosophy became one of two major, long-term initiatives embarked upon by the Nazis for the entirety of their time in power. Anti-Semitic policies began within the first months of the Third Reich and accelerated until the fall of Nazi Germany in 1945. In the end, six million Jews were killed in the Holocaust, and millions more were displaced. The attempted extermination of Europe's Jews did not happen overnight, however. Instead, Jewish persecution proceeded in stages, escalating in intensity as time went on and as conditions allowed. It was only after the start of World War II that the Nazis strove for a larger, permanent solution to the "Jewish problem."

Anti-Semitic sentiment first found legislative expression in measures designed to persecute and stigmatize the Jewish population of Germany. Jewish judges were dismissed on March 31, 1933, and the following day a nationwide boycott of Jewish businesses began. On April 7, Jews were banned from the civil service, and on April 25, enrollment of non-Aryans in schools was capped at 1.5 percent. Jewish doctors were prevented from practicing on non-Jewish women, and Jews were treated as outsiders in almost all aspects of their daily lives, forced to wear a yellow star so they could be easily identified. In 1935, the Nuremberg Laws were passed, which codified anti-Semitism in an unprecedented fashion. The Law for the Protection of German Blood and Honor forbade Jews from marrying or having relationships with Gentiles, and the Reich Citizenship Law provided a pseudo-scientific definition of who was or was not Jewish. Under the law, any German with three or four Jewish grandparents was considered a Jew, and only those with no Jewish grandparents were considered to be purely German. The law stripped those defined as Jews of their citizenship, a major escalation in Nazi anti-Semitism. The state had no obligation to secure any rights for non-citizens, meaning that Jews now had no legal standing to fight back against discrimination. Over the next few years, sporadic violence against Jews took place, as well as deportations to concentration camps, where Jews were forced to work.

In 1938, the son of a deported Jew assassinated a German official in Paris, sparking a further escalation in Nazi persecution. Seizing on the assassination as proof that Jews were inherently dangerous, the Nazis began to openly encourage widespread violence. Jewish homes, businesses, and synagogues were targeted for destruction, and Jews were attacked in the streets by crowds of angry Germans. Thousands of Jews were rounded up and sent to concentration camps, while thousands more fled the country. Beginning in 1939, as more and more Jews came under German control, a policy of ghettoization was put in place. Sections of various cities were sealed off with fencing and barbed wire, and Jews were herded into them. Conditions were terrible, with many Jews in the ghettos dying of starvation. Living space was extremely cramped, as the ghettos usually only comprised a few blocks and contained hundreds of thousands of people. The largest ghetto, in Warsaw, Poland, saw almost half a million Jews crammed into less than 2 square miles (5.2 square kilometers).

The last escalation in the German campaign against the Jews came in 1942, with the development of the Final Solution and the construction of the death camps. Upon the invasion of the Soviet Union the year before, German soldiers had been ordered to begin executing Jews on sight. Hitler viewed all of the peoples of the East, whether Jewish or not, as a surplus population. The Nazis, therefore, had no need

KRISTALLNACHT

A man cleans up after Kristallnacht.

Kristallnacht, the Night of Broken Glass, was one of the largest attacks on Jewish citizens and property in Germany before the outbreak of World War II. The attacks took the form of a pogrom, like those that had riven Eastern Europe in the late nineteenth and early twentieth centuries. It also represented an escalation in the persecution of Jews in Nazi Germany. Before *Kristallnacht*, most anti-Semitic discrimination took the form of bureaucratic and legal restrictions (the Nuremberg Laws being the prime example). The Kristallnacht pogrom marked the beginning of a period of widespread violence that would eventually lead to the Holocaust.

On the night of November 9, 1938, Jewish homes and businesses were attacked and plundered and their windows were shattered. Synagogues were ransacked and burned, and Jewish citizens were insulted, humiliated, and beaten in the streets. While the attacks were organized and sanctioned by the Nazis, German citizens also took part. Classes of schoolchildren were brought out by their teachers to participate, troops of Hitler Youth were deployed, and ordinary bystanders egged on the violence and took part in the looting. Joseph Goebbels himself wandered the streets of Munich as the pogrom was under way, inciting the people he encountered to go further in their destruction.

The nationwide pogrom, organized by and perpetrated with the consent of the state, made widespread violence against Jewish individuals and businesses more openly acceptable and laid the groundwork for further state oppression.

for the Jews even as labor, making them entirely expendable. In the second half of 1941 alone, one million Jews were shot dead. By early 1942, new methods were sought to dispose of Jews more effectively.

Building on the rationalization and efficiency-driven procedures that had made Weimar industry so successful during the mid-1920s, the Nazis settled on the idea of gas chambers to wipe out Europe's Jews en masse with little effort. Installed at a handful of camps around Eastern Europe, the gas chambers turned murder into an industry. The ghettos were liquidated, their Jewish prisoners loaded onto cattle cars and taken to Auschwitz and other death camps. There, they were either worked to death or sent straight to the gas chamber. Three million Jews were killed in the first year alone, and by 1945 the Holocaust had claimed six million Jewish lives, over 60 percent of European Jewry. In addition

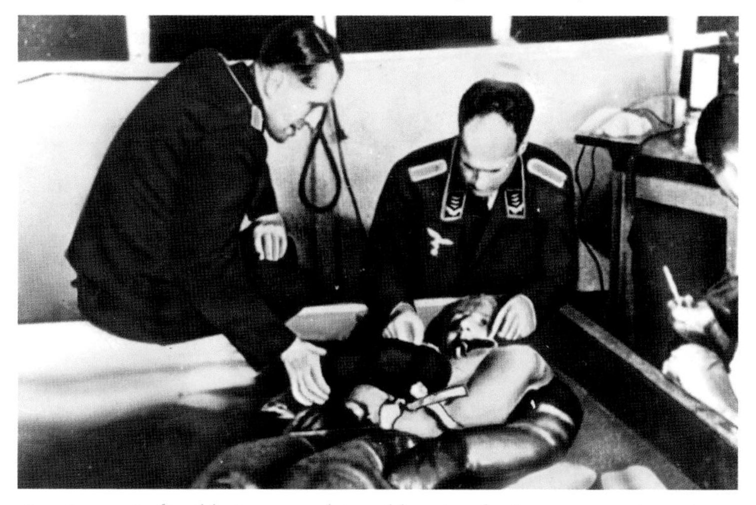

A prisoner is forcibly immersed in cold water during an experiment at Dachau concentration camp, one of many brutalities committed during the Holocaust.

to the Jews, the Nazi extermination policies also targeted gypsies, homosexuals, Slavs, the aged, and the mentally ill. Over twelve million people in total were murdered during the Holocaust.

The Road to World War II

At the same time that the Nazis were pursuing policies of racial purification, the state was also preparing to meet Hitler's other major goal: the acquisition of additional territories into which the German race could expand and multiply. Having already declared that *lebensraum* could be found in the lands to the east, Hitler knew that Germany needed to build up its strength before launching an attack. Therefore, in the early years of the Third Reich, he pursued a cautious foreign policy that was largely conciliatory to the other European powers. This was a ruse from the start, as Hitler never had any intention of actually maintaining peace on the continent, but it served to buy time while the German military was rebuilt. It also allowed the Nazis to conduct negotiations with the other nations of Europe, securing alliances with some and attempting to isolate others.

The most obvious ally was Fascist Italy under Benito Mussolini. Italian Fascism and German National Socialism were very similar ideologies, and the two leaders had personal respect for one another. Hitler admired Mussolini and what he had achieved, and Mussolini was quick to congratulate Hitler on the day he was appointed chancellor. France, meanwhile, was a particularly potent enemy in Hitler's mind, due to its historical rivalry with Germany. Hitler blamed France more than any of the other Allied powers for Germany's treatment after World War I, and France was believed to be the one European power that could offer real resistance to the Nazis once they started their war. The Soviet Union was also a particular target of hatred for Hitler, as it represented a combination of all the forces he most loathed: the Russian people were ethnically Slavs, many were Jewish, and the government was Marxist.

At the same time that Hitler was endeavoring to maintain temporary stability in Europe, he was also withdrawing Germany from its international commitments. Hitler preferred bilateral agreements, those between only two countries, as they were easier to break. Multilateral agreements and alliances, including the League of Nations, were far harder to break without suffering major consequences. Germany had only been admitted to the League in 1926, but Hitler nonetheless withdrew from the international body in October 1933. By this time, foreign condemnation of the new regime had begun to pour in. The Nazis' crackdown on opposition parties, curtailment of civil liberties, dismissal of academics, and harsh anti-Semitic practices had all come in for criticism from Europe and the United States. In the face of this growing hostility, Hitler offered some token excuses for Nazi policies and decided to limit the amount of publicity that German rearmament received. Privately, he told his generals in February 1934 that the military needed to be prepared to fight a defensive war within five years, and ready to launch an offensive war within eight.

BENITO MUSSOLINI AND ITALIAN FASCISM

Born on July 29, 1883, Benito Mussolini was a temperamental man who was ruled by his passions and often used violence to pursue his desires. Though he began his political career as a socialist, as time went on, his political views began to shift, ultimately leading to his expulsion from the Socialist Party when he enthusiastically supported World War I.

After serving in the war, Mussolini formed the Fascist Party in 1919. Originally conceived of as a program of action rather than a defined ideology, Italian Fascism came to articulate the position that an individual should be allowed freedom only insofar as it did not interfere with the greater good of the state. Like the Fascism of the Nazis, Italian Fascism sought to unite people along purely national lines, and was anti-democratic, arguing for rule by one strong leader. The ephemeral nature of Italian Fascism, which embraced feelings and beliefs rather than concrete policy proposals, was very similar to German Nazism.

The Fascists were elected to the Italian government in 1921. In 1922, with Italy descending into political chaos, Mussolini and his Black Shirts (an armed paramilitary formation much like Hitler's SA) marched on Rome. Upon arrival, Mussolini claimed that he was the only man capable of restoring order to Italy. King Victor Emmanuel III, like Hindenburg in Germany, thought he could use Mussolini to maintain stability and prevent a civil war. He allowed Mussolini to form a government, albeit one which quickly began dispensing with the trappings of democracy. By 1925, Mussolini was governing as a dictator. Often referred to as *Il Duce* (The Leader), Mussolini ruled through strong state control and intimidation. His Fascist dictatorship later served as a model for Hitler, and the two men became friends, their shared ideologies forming the foundations of an alliance that would last through World War II.

The pace of remilitarization more than met these goals. A new conscription law was passed in 1935, flouting the Treaty of Versailles. The next year, in March, the German military reoccupied the Rhineland. This westernmost region of Germany bordered France and Belgium, and the Treaty of Versailles had mandated that it be utterly demilitarized. These aggressive violations of the treaty were indicative of Germany's defiant attitude toward international law, but little attention was paid to them—the Rhineland was reoccupied at the same time that a Fascist movement was being countered in France and shortly before civil war erupted in Spain. The Spanish Civil War offered Hitler an opportunity to test the strength of his new military. The Nazis and the Italian Fascists provided equipment and troops to the Spanish Nationalists, led by the right-wing general Francisco Franco, and supported his eventual victory. With the German military proving adequate, Hitler was ready to begin expansion.

The first step was taken on March 12, 1938, with the **annexation** of Austria. Known as the *Anschluss,* the German seizure of its southern neighbor was largely bloodless, greeted with enthusiasm by the Austrian people, and a long time coming.

Hitler had been born in Austria and had always considered it to be a part of Germany. He thought of the Austrian people as part of the German race, and the first phase in his plan for foreign conquest was uniting all the German peoples that lived outside of the Reich. Many Austrian citizens desired the same thing, and the Anschluss was celebrated on both sides of the former border.

From Austria, Hitler's attention turned to Czechoslovakia. Many ethnic Germans lived in the Sudetenland, the region of the country that shared a border with Germany, and Hitler wished to incorporate them into his Reich. More broadly, he believed that the country of Czechoslovakia as a whole occupied historically German lands that needed to be brought into the German state. Agitating for the Sudetenland first, the Nazis staged a series of incidents along the German-Czech border to justify their annexation of the territory. The international community was unsure how to respond to the Sudeten Crisis. All parties wanted to avoid war, but Germany was violating the territorial integrity of her neighbor, again in violation of the terms of the Treaty of Versailles. A series of meetings were held, the outcome of which seemed to maintain peace. The Sudetenland was legally transferred to Germany, and Hitler promised not to take any further territory. This promise was immediately broken, as preparations for the invasion of the rest of Czechoslovakia began the very next day, and Germany rolled through the country in March 1939.

Events moved quickly following the invasion. The military alliance between Germany and Italy was formalized, as was an opposing alliance between France and Britain. The most shocking agreement made in 1939, however, came between Germany and the Soviet Union. The Molotov-Ribbentrop Pact, signed in August, was not an alliance but rather a nonaggression pact. Germany and the Soviet Union were not obliged to support one another in any military endeavors, but the pact did foreclose on the possibility of war between them. The international community was stunned by the agreement. Germany hated the Soviet Union, was staunchly anti-Communist, and Hitler's racial view of the world cast nearly everyone living in Russia as inherently inferior. Why would these two powers agree to this? The answer was expedience. Joseph Stalin, leader of the Soviet Union, had spent the 1930s attempting to form alliances with Britain and France, to counter the rising threat of Nazi Germany. Neither state trusted him though, wary of Communism as an ideology and Stalin as a man. With no other options, Stalin agreed to negotiate with Hitler in order to forestall war.

For his part, Hitler was happy to make a temporary peace with the Soviet Union, as it would allow him to wage war with France without having to worry about the Red Army invading Germany from the east. Hitler never intended to abide by the pact long-term, nor did Stalin expect him to. For the time being, however, the pact was advantageous for both parties. Hitler could launch his war more easily, and Stalin had more time to prepare his forces for the inevitable Nazi betrayal.

On September 1, 1939, the Nazis invaded Poland. Britain and France declared war on Germany in response, and World War II had officially begun. The war would last six years and cost millions of lives and, together with the Holocaust, fundamentally change the world forever. The rise of the Nazis in Germany resulted in death, destruction, and pure evil on a scale unprecedented in human history, and the legacy of their twelve years in power continues to impact the world today.

N.S.M.

5

Modern Fascism: The Legacy of the Nazis

The defeat of the Nazis in 1945 brought an end to the Holocaust and peace to the European theater of World War II. It was not, however, a permanent defeat of Fascism. The ideology that had driven the Nazis, the Italian Fascists, and various other movements across Europe lingered, and continues to have echoes today.

In the seven decades since the Nazis were deposed, Fascist ideology has gone through a number of transformations and has broken with Nazism in some significant respects. Changing political and social conditions throughout the Western world precipitated these breaks, as politicians of the extreme right have had to adjust their rhetoric and political programs to remain electorally viable. Even so, core Fascist tenets of extreme national glorification and demonization

Opposite: *An American neo-Nazi attends a Ku Klux Klan demonstration in Columbia, South Carolina, in 2015.*

of "outsiders" remain at the heart of many parties on the far right in Europe. Whether or not it is fair to label these parties "Fascist" is a matter of disagreement, but it is clear that the fears and prejudices tapped into by the Nazis are not unique to the 1920s and 1930s, and parties of the extreme right can still exploit these fears to gain power.

Suppression and Survival

One major reason for the shifting of the political right away from explicit Fascism over the last fifty years was how thoroughly discredited the ideology became after World War II. The Nazis were rigorously stripped of power by the victorious Allies, and thousands of trials were held for former Nazi officials and party functionaries. The Allies sought to thoroughly eradicate Nazism from Germany, with particularly harsh purges of Nazis taking place in the Soviet-occupied zone. Elsewhere in Europe, newly liberated states dealt with Fascists within their borders just as strictly. In Norway and the Netherlands, Fascist Party members and Nazi collaborators were uniformly brought up on charges and punished, with sentences ranging from fines to execution. Those who escaped jail time were nevertheless prevented from playing any prominent role in politics or polite society ever again. There was slightly more forgiveness in Eastern Europe, where low-level functionaries were allowed to join the Communist Party, but high-ranking party members met a grim fate in the territories occupied by the Soviet Union.

The ideology of the Nazis was consistently condemned throughout Europe, and has remained toxic to this day. Many countries, especially those that were most directly affected by the war and the Holocaust, have passed laws expressly forbidding Holocaust denial and the resurfacing of Nazism. While some of these states apply the laws sparingly, others are far stricter. In Germany, the Nazi Party has been branded a criminal organization and banned; also prohibited is the display of Nazi symbols, any written materials or images that promote Nazi ideology, and the denial of the Holocaust. In Austria, denying the Holocaust or performing activities inspired by the Nazis are offenses punishable by a prison term of up to ten years, and French law makes it an offense to question the existence of "crimes against humanity," as they are defined by the Nuremberg Charter.

While proponents of these laws argue that as time goes on it becomes increasingly important to prosecute the kind of hate speech that could potentially allow for a resurgence of Nazism, opponents have concerns about the restrictions the laws place on free speech. Many nations, including the United States, the United Kingdom, and the countries of Scandinavia, do not have any laws banning Nazi symbols or ideology, taking the position that such laws would violate a person's right to free expression. Those who argue against anti-Nazi legislation make the point that the government being able to criminalize certain forms of political speech, however odious, is a dangerous precedent to set, and one that can be easily abused. Free speech advocates also point out that putting a Holocaust denier on public trial can actually *raise* his or her profile, exposing more people to the exact views that the state is trying to suppress.

The futility of trying to outlaw an idea can be seen in the resilience of Fascism within Germany. Despite the harsh laws aimed at ridding the country of Nazism, a small percentage of the country remains drawn toward the ideology. The neo-Nazi groups that exist in Germany attract mostly disaffected young people and vary in terms of their extremity. Some primarily exist to spread anti-Semitic and racist propaganda, while others go beyond propagandizing and commit murder and other acts of violence. The government has banned several neo-Nazi organizations, partly in an effort to make it easier to prosecute individual members, but new organizations simply emerge to take their place. The internet provides neo-Nazis a means of avoiding German censorship laws, and neo-Nazi music, laced with anti-Semitic and racist messages, is an effective way of spreading Fascist propaganda. The German government has taken steps to silence this music, from banning individual songs to jailing neo-Nazi musicians, but they have been unsuccessful in preventing its proliferation.

In the political realm, the torch of Fascism is carried by the far-right National Democratic Party (NPD). The NPD is the party of choice for Germany's neo-Nazis and has encouraged the support of these groups by distributing neo-Nazi music for free outside of schools. While the NPD holds no seats at the national level, it does have a presence in state and local councils. Multiple attempts have been made to ban the party, but they have so far proved unsuccessful.

Neo-Fascism

The presence of neo-Nazis and the NPD in Germany shows that Fascism cannot simply be legislated away. It also demonstrates, however, that Fascism as a concept has become incredibly toxic in the modern world, and appeals only to a small fringe. What is to be made, then, of the rise of numerous parties and politicians across Europe and the United States that have been labeled "neo-Fascist"?

Despite widespread revulsion for Fascism as a political movement, many animating elements of Fascist ideology have been brought out of the fringes and into the mainstream. The politicians and parties responsible for this resurrection have been able to accomplish it by successfully articulating old grievances in new language. The neo-Fascists of Europe and the United States have done away with the elements of Fascism that are no longer politically acceptable while maintaining those that continue to motivate a base of voters. The ability of these figures to wrap a set of popular, seemingly democratic policies around a core of far right ethnonationalism has dramatically shifted the political calculus on both sides of the Atlantic in the last decade.

Neo-Fascism is today characterized most clearly by an intense hostility to immigration, usually predicated on the grounds that immigrants are lowering the material and cultural quality of life of the native population. This is obviously similar to the racial purity espoused by Mussolini's Fascism or Hitler's National Socialism, but also points to some key differences with the past, and areas in which neo-Fascism has adapted. The racial "science" that informed Hitler's worldview has been utterly discredited, so modern Fascists instead look at the world through the lenses of nationality, culture, and religion. The community that Fascism seeks to protect and restore to greatness (in Hitler's conception, the Aryan race) is now generally identified along national lines—the American people, the French people, the Dutch people, etc. The outsiders that are blamed for society's ills are no longer races but other nationalities, religions, or cultures.

In Europe, the current influx of migrants and refugees from the Middle East as a result of the War on Terror has led numerous figures on the far right to speak out about what they see as the dangers of "Muslim culture" and its perceived incongruity with Western values. In this way, the core goal of Fascism is carried on in a way that is compatible with the modern political climate: an argument is made for the preservation of a national group at the expense of another group that is perceived to be foreign. Instead of making distinctions based on biological racism, however, modern-day Fascists focus their prejudice on culture and nationality. This allows neo-Fascists to express the same bigotry and hostility toward those who are different as their historical predecessors, without suffering from the stigma that comes along with Nazism or explicit racism.

The embrace of a national culture by neo-Fascists points to other divergences from earlier forms of Fascism. Contemporary calls for unity and harsh restrictions on immigration have challenged the previous Fascist quest for

Protestors demonstrate against rising Fascist sentiments in the United States on January 20, 2017.

territorial expansion. Both Hitler and Mussolini longed to expand into other lands, while neo-Fascists instead argue for tougher enforcement of existing borders. Neo-Fascists are also more committed to democracy than their historical predecessors. Part of Hitler's appeal was his deep-seated hatred of the Weimar Republic and his promise to replace it with autocratic rule. Modern-day Fascists, by comparison, are far more willing to work within the system. They may want to fundamentally alter which citizens the government is responsive to, but they do not want to destroy the government itself.

These changes have allowed Fascism to survive into the contemporary era, where it is making a political resurgence. Neo-Fascist parties have been gaining in popularity over the last decade in both Europe and the United States, their success based in large part on two key events: the global War on Terror and the economic recession of 2008. The War on Terror, begun in the weeks following the September 11, 2001, terrorist attacks in the United States, has caused tremendous instability in the Middle East. Over the course of the war, millions of refugees have fled the region, many ending up in Europe or the United States. There, they have found themselves targets of the political right, demonized as potential terrorists by parties and politicians who do not care to distinguish between an ordinary Muslim and an Islamic fundamentalist. These politicians argue that Muslim immigrants represent an alien culture, one that will never be compatible with that of the West. They also describe Muslim immigration as harmful to native Europeans, claiming that social welfare programs are being overwhelmed and that secular values are under attack. The prescription offered for these problems is a drastic reduction, if not outright halt, of immigration of certain peoples, and a reemphasis of the primacy of the native population in all matters.

Sowing fear of foreigners and offering scapegoats for societal problems is not a technique exclusive to Fascists, of course. It is a tactic employed by parties across the political spectrum, and does not by itself account for the growing popularity of neo-Fascist politicians. When the 2008 economic crash is taken into account, however, the picture becomes clearer, and parallels with Weimar Germany sharpen.

The financial crisis of 2008, much like the Great Depression of 1929, began in the United States and spread to the rest of the world. While the economic downturn was not as severe, there were nonetheless long-lasting consequences in the form of lost jobs, rising unemployment, and stagnant wages. The recovery, when it eventually came, was sluggish and disproportionately beneficial to wealthy individuals. In the years since the crisis, material conditions for the lower and middle classes have remained largely unchanged, and governments have failed to adequately address this problem. A wave of anti-establishment sentiment has built up, which has been seized on by the parties of the extreme right. Since these politicians and parties have largely existed outside of the political mainstream, they are able to offer a credible critique of the government and present a genuine alternative. Positioning themselves as **populists**, they promise to change how—and for whom—the government operates. Just as the Nazis were able to use the crisis of the Great Depression and the paralysis of the major Weimar parties that followed as an opportunity to attract voters to their cause, so too have modern neo-Fascists taken advantage of the global financial meltdown and the subsequent disillusionment with established politicians to sell themselves as the only real alternative. This combination of anti-establishment, economic populism and anti-immigrant, xenophobic nationalism has proven to be a potent one, and it offers a message that mainstream parties struggle to counter.

Neo-Fascist Movements and Politicians

In the Netherlands, the face of neo-Fascism is currently Geert Wilders, head of the Party for Freedom (PVV). Originally a libertarian conservative, Wilders's career was changed by two high-profile assassinations in the early 2000s. Today, he is one of the most prominent anti-Muslim voices in the country. He

COMPARING FASCISM AND NEO-FASCISM

Fascism has evolved since the 1930s, navigating shifting political climates and making certain changes in order to remain a viable political force. Some major similarities and differences between Fascism and neo-Fascism are listed below.

Similarities

- Central belief in the inherent superiority of a particular group of people, and a desire to unite said group and restore it to a point of prosperity and glory that (theoretically) once existed.
- Intense hatred for groups deemed inferior, and belief that these "lower" groups are responsible for the diminished prosperity of the "higher" group.
- Disdain for established politicians and parties, and presentation as a genuine alternative to the traditional political system.
- A tendency to organize behind one charismatic leader.
- Emphasis is placed on law, order, stability, and deference to authority.

Differences

- Traditional Fascism based its classification of peoples on race and theories of "racial science" that have since been discredited. Neo-Fascists delineate peoples' relative worth based on nationality, religion, and/or culture.
- Fascism was militarily aggressive and sought to expand the borders of the state. Neo-Fascism is concerned with enforcing existing borders and generally has no desire for territorial expansion.
- Fascists called for an end to democracy and the establishment of an authoritarian form of government. Neo-Fascists are usually willing to work within existing democratic structures and do not advocate for their destruction.
- Fascist organizations of the past generally contained a paramilitary force and met political opponents with violence. Neo-Fascists do not employ political violence in anything close to the same way.
- Fascists were extremely culturally conservative (anti-women, anti-LGBT, etc.). Some neo-Fascists have begun to abandon these values, though this is entirely dependent on the particular party and politician.

claims that Islam is incompatible with Dutch values and that the socially liberal gains made by the Dutch people need to be protected from conservative Muslim ideology. Wilders has managed to position himself as an advocate for Jews, women, and the LGBT community, claiming that the true threat to these minority groups comes from Islam. He has also come out against the mainstream parties, arguing that they have prioritized giving benefits to immigrants over ensuring the material security of the Dutch people. The combination of Wilders's anti-establishment, anti-immigrant message and his appearance as a protector of the ordinary Dutch citizen has led to electoral victories for the PVV, among them a second-place finish in the 2017 parliamentary elections.

Wilders and the PVV also have international ties, their closest ally being the National Front (FN) party in France. The National Front was formed in 1972 as an offshoot of another neo-Fascist organization and was designed to be more palatable to the French public. Chosen to lead the FN was Jean-Marie Le Pen, a war veteran, who it was thought would be able to attract new voters to the party. The National Front began emphasizing immigration as a key issue under Le Pen's leadership, with Le Pen himself saying that "the flourishing of nations is best accomplished on their own territory." Le Pen also diminished the Holocaust, calling the gas chambers a mere "detail of the history of World War II." Between remarks of this sort and the association of the FN with neo-Nazi groups in France, the party's attempt to distance itself from the more repellant aspects of Fascism proved a failure. That changed in 2011, however, when the party was taken over by Marine Le Pen, Jean-Marie's daughter. Under her leadership, the FN has rejected the more noxious elements of its past and has managed to become a mainstream party within France. Like Wilders, Le Pen has embraced economically populist positions while attacking immigration as the cause of France's problems. This tactic has proved successful, as numerous local races have been won by FN candidates and Marine Le Pen is now a frontrunner in the presidential elections in 2017.

Other European neo-Fascist parties have been less concerned with improving their image. The Svoboda Party in Ukraine has been condemned by the European Union but has continued to remain popular and hold seats in Ukraine's parliament. The Golden Dawn Party in Greece is perhaps the most blatantly neo-Fascist party in all of Europe; its logo bears a disquieting resemblance to a swastika, and the party's founder, Nikolaos Michaloliakos, has been recorded making a Nazi salute and denying the Holocaust. In Slovakia, the far right People's Party, "Our Slovakia," won 8 percent of the vote in the 2016 elections, giving them fourteen seats in the National Council. Support for the People's Party came heavily from the young, a trend that is consistent across Europe: the National Front in France and the PVV in the Netherlands also draw significant support from younger generations. This lies in stark contrast to the United States, where young Americans skew overwhelmingly to the left.

A demonstration by the Golden Dawn Party in Greece in September 2016

The Far-Right Ascendant

Today, far-right influences are being felt strongly within political spheres in the United States and around the world. In 2016, Republican nominee Donald Trump was elected president of the United States after running a campaign that embraced certain far-right positions and techniques. For instance, Trump exercised xenophobia as part of his campaign, targeting Muslims and Latin Americans. He promised to ban Muslims from entering the country and enact stricter surveillance measures on Muslim citizens. As for Latino immigrants, he pledged to construct a wall along the US–Mexico border and deport undocumented residents. Trump blamed immigrants for taking American jobs and changing

American culture for the worse, and presented himself as a figure capable of reversing both trends. Like the parties of the extreme right in Europe, Trump wed this xenophobic nationalism with anti-establishment, populist rhetoric. He disdained the elite figures of both major American political parties and claimed to speak for the average American citizen.

Other victories for the far right have come through referendums in Europe. The decision for the United Kingdom to leave the European Union in June 2016 (the "Brexit" vote) was supported most heavily by the United Kingdom Independence Party (UKIP), a right-wing party led at the time by Nigel Farage. He claimed that the free movement of peoples guaranteed by the European Union was resulting in too much immigration to Britain and that business regulations and other rules set out by the EU were preventing the country from governing its own affairs. These claims were in line with the appeals of the European neo-Fascists, although not quite as extreme in tone. Following the referendum, British prime minister David Cameron (who had supported remaining in the European Union) resigned, and the more conservative Theresa May took his seat.

A similar fate befell the Italian prime minister Matteo Renzi in a December 2016 referendum. Renzi had proposed a constitutional amendment that would have reduced the number of legislators in the Italian senate. His opponents on both the right and left saw this as a power grab, and the referendum was overwhelmingly defeated, becoming a vote against Renzi as much as it was a vote against the amendment. The extreme right throughout Europe celebrated Renzi's defeat and subsequent resignation, with Marine Le Pen calling it a signal to France to reject similar politicians.

With these victories, it is clear that a new trend is emerging. Fifteen years after the start of the War on Terror and ten years after the global financial crisis, resentment at the established political order is building. Just as the Great Depression allowed long-simmering discontent with the Weimar Republic to boil over and express itself with support for a Fascist party, so too have the crises of the last two decades allowed for the growth of a new kind of Fascism.

Dispensing with the elements of Nazism that are no longer politically acceptable, neo-Fascists have managed to maintain the core elements of the old ideology—the necessity of the supremacy of a particular people and hatred for outsiders—and unite them with populist, anti-establishment rhetoric. This combination has proved potent, as neo-Fascists are able to successfully pin economic and social problems on immigrants and those deemed foreign, while also promising to throw out the current political class and replace it with one that will be more responsive to "the people," a term which in this context excludes significant portions of the population.

In both Europe and the United States, the parties of the mainstream left and right have become tied to an increasingly unpopular political system of which they can offer no substantive critique. As the architects of the policies that have shaped the last fifteen years, the established parties have no real answer for the harm that has been caused as a result, or solutions for those that have been left behind. In depression-era Germany, the lack of solutions from the traditional parties prompted a shift in support toward the Nazis, and a similar political shift is taking place today. Unless a genuine, credible alternative to neo-Fascism is provided, one that can address the failings of the modern political order without compromising on its commitments to democracy, freedom, diversity, equality, and justice, it is likely that history will repeat itself, and the world will see a new rise of the extreme right.

annexation The assumption of political control of a region that had previously been either self-governed or administered by another state.

anti-Semitism Hatred, prejudice, or discrimination against Jews.

coalition A group of political parties that work together as a united front within a parliamentary government.

Communism A political, economic, and social ideology aimed at establishing a society in which the people control the means of production and social classes are eliminated.

Expressionism An artistic movement of the early twentieth century that sought to examine the psychological depths of individuals and societies and represent emotional states rather than physical reality.

Fascism A system of political and social organization aimed at restoring a specific group of people to a level of prosperity and glory that has been lost due to the actions of a minority group or groups; in practice, Fascism is characterized by aggressive nationalism, racism, xenophobia, hostility to democracy, political violence, and strict enforcement of traditional values and morals.

hyperinflation The increasingly rapid rise in the price of goods and services in a particular economy, quickly devaluing the currency.

ideologue A person who follows an ideology blindly.

inflation The sustained increase in the price level of goods and services over a period of time, resulting in the loss of value of a particular currency.

kaiser The German term for emperor, the imperial ruler of pre–Weimar Germany.

lebensraum "Living space," the term used by Hitler to describe the lands in Eastern Europe that he wanted to conquer so as to allow the German race to flourish.

militarism The belief of a state or a people that the maintenance of a strong, well-respected military and its aggressive use to advance national interests is of the utmost importance.

nationalism The feeling of intense pride in and love for one's nation, which can be defined in terms of geography, race, ethnicity, or culture.

neo-Fascism The modern version of Fascism, which continues to stress the supremacy of a particular group of people and the inferiority of others, though other characteristics of Fascism may be downplayed or abandoned altogether.

paramilitary A force organized and trained as an army that exists separately from a state's formal armed forces.

plebiscite A vote in which the electorate is given the option to support or oppose a particular proposal; also known as a referendum.

pogrom A violent attack on Jewish individuals or Jewish-owned property, with the intent of intimidating or persecuting Jews.

populism A political course of action that appeals to the broad mass of voters while disdaining elite individuals in government and the private sector; populism can be left-wing or right-wing.

putsch A coup, the seizure of political power in a state through illegal and usually violent means.

reparations A form of restitution for acts of injustice, given to the victim by the perpetrator.

social democracy A political, economic, and social ideology that seeks to regulate a capitalist economy, nationalize certain industries, and maintain a strong social welfare state in an effort to achieve social justice and greater equality.

xenophobia The fear of people or cultures that are perceived to be foreign.

1889 Adolf Hitler is born.

1914 Start of World War I.

1918 World War I ends; German Revolution begins and the kaiser abdicates his throne.

1919 Founding of the Weimar Republic and suppression of Communist revolt; the Treaty of Versailles is drafted and signed; Hitler joins the German Worker's Party (DAP).

1920 The DAP becomes the National Socialist German Worker's Party (NSDAP), commonly referred to as the Nazi Party; Hitler becomes a major figure within the party; release of *The Cabinet of Dr. Caligari.*

1921 Reparations bill delivered to the Weimar Republic; existing inflation begins to worsen.

1922 Inflation turns into hyperinflation; Mussolini and the Fascists come to power in Italy.

1923 Hyperinflation crisis reaches its peak; the Nazi Beer Hall Putsch is defeated.

1924 Hitler is sentenced to prison, where he writes *Mein Kampf.*

1925 Paul von Hindenburg is elected German president; publication of *Mein Kampf.*

1929 The Great Depression begins.

1930 Heinrich Brüning begins ruling Germany by decree; the Nazis are elected to the Reichstag in significant numbers.

1931 The Social Democrats (SPD) begin pursuing a policy of toleration toward Brüning's government.

1932 Hindenburg reelected president; Brüning replaced as chancellor with Franz von Papen; Hitler denied the chancellery; the Nazis lose seats in November elections.

1933 Adolf Hitler appointed chancellor of Germany.

1934 Nazi Blood Purge; Hitler assumes the presidency.

1935 Nuremberg Laws passed; release of *The Triumph of the Will*, directed by Leni Riefenstahl.

1936 Remilitarization of the Rhineland; Spanish Civil War begins.

1938 Germany annexes Austria; *Kristallnacht*; Sudeten crisis resolves in Hitler's favor; release of *Olympia.*

1939 Nazi invasion of Czechoslovakia; Molotov-Ribbentrop Pact; Germany invades Poland; World War II begins.

1942 Final Solution to exterminate European Jews begins.

1945 Nazi Germany is defeated in World War II; death of Hitler; the Holocaust ends.

Books

Hitler, Adolf. *Mein Kampf.* Translated by Ralph Manheim. Boston, MA: Houghton Mifflin, 1998.

Ullrich, Volker. *Hitler: Ascent, 1889–1939.* Translated by Jefferson Chase. New York: Knopf, 2016.

Weitz, Eric D. *Weimar Germany: Promise and Tragedy.* 2nd ed. Princeton, NJ: Princeton University Press, 2013.

Websites/Organizations

United States Holocaust Memorial Museum

http://www.ushmm.org

The Holocaust Memorial Museum website contains a wealth of resources, including primary documents, testimonies of Holocaust survivors, and an encyclopedia that details events before, during, and after the rise of the Nazi Party.

Yad Vashem

http://www.yadvashem.org

Like the US Holocaust Memorial Museum, Yad Vashem acts as a memorial to the victims of the Holocaust as well as an educational resource; the website offers written and video material on the progression of the Holocaust in addition to databases of individual deportations and names of victims.

Videos

Apocalypse: The Rise of Hitler

http://www.youtube.com/watch?v=L9waMqzl3Ro

Featuring authentic, first-hand footage and rare photographs, this documentary takes an in-depth look at Hitler's activities during World War I, his developing ideology, and the formation and growth of the Nazi Party.

The Cabinet of Dr. Caligari (1920)

The prime example of German Expressionism in cinema, *The Cabinet of Dr. Caligari* employs startling visuals, exaggerated set design, and innovative lighting to tell a haunting story.

Triumph of the Will (1935)

http://www.youtube.com/watch?v=GHs2coAzLJ8

Going down in cinematic history as one of the most famous propaganda films of all time, Leni Riefenstahl's first major documentary project for Hitler offers a glimpse of Nazi Germany in its early years.

Cook, David A. *A History of Narrative Film*. 4th ed. New York: W.W. Norton & Company, 2004.

Copsey, Nigel. "'Fascism… but with an open mind.' Reflections on the Contemporary FarRight in (Western) Europe." *Fascism* 2, no. 1 (2013): 1-17.

Dobkowski, Michael N., and Isidor Wallimann, eds. *Towards the Holocaust: The Social and Economic Collapse of the Weimar Republic*. Westport: Greenwood Press, 1983. http://surface.syr.edu/books/17.

Giroux, Henry A. "Fascism in Donald Trump's United States." *Truthout*, December 8, 2015. http://www.truth-out.org/news/item/33951-fascism-in-donald-trump-s-united-states.

Hitler, Adolf. *Mein Kampf.* Translated by James Murphy. London, UK: Hurst & Blackett, 1939; Project Gutenberg, 2002. http://gutenberg.net.au/ebooks02/0200601.txt.

Kallis, Aristotle. "When Fascism Became Mainstream: The Challenge of Extremism in Times of Crisis." *Fascism* 4, no. 1 (2015): 1-24.

King, Gary, Ori Rosen, Martin Tanner, and Alexander F. Wagner. "Ordinary Economic Voting Behavior in the Extraordinary Election of Adolf Hitler." *Journal of Economic History* 68, no. 4 (December 2008): 951-996. http://nrs.harvard.edu/urn-3:HUL.InstRepos:3443107.

Laqueur, Walter. *Fascism: Past, Present, Future*. Oxford, UK: Oxford University Press, 1996. Pine, Lisa, ed. *Life and Times in Nazi Germany*. New York: Bloomsbury, 2016.

Polakow-Suransky, Sasha. "The Ruthlessly Effective Rebranding of Europe's New Far Right."*Guardian*, November 1, 2016. http://www.theguardian.com/world/2016/nov/01/the-ruthlessly-effective-rebranding-of-europes-new-far-right.

Schleunes, Karl A. *The Twisted Road to Auschwitz: Nazi Policy Toward German Jews, 1933–1939*. Chicago: University of Illinois Press, 1990.

Shirer, William L. *The Rise and Fall of Adolf Hitler*. New York: RosettaBooks, 2013.Kindle edition.

Steinweis, Alan E. *Kristallnacht 1938*. Cambridge, UK: Belknap Press, 2009.

Weinberg, Gerhard L. *Hitler's Foreign Policy 1933–1939: The Road to World War II*. New York: Enigma Books, 2010.

Weitz, Eric D. *Weimar Germany: Promise and Tragedy*. 2d ed. Princeton, NJ: Princeton University Press, 2013. Kindle edition.

Page numbers in **boldface** are illustrations. Entries in **boldface** are glossary terms.

Brett Griffin earned a degree in history from Canisius College, with a focus on American and European history. The first half of the twentieth century, including the world wars and the years between, is the time period about which he is most fascinated. In addition to history, Griffin is also passionate about film, music, and literature, and enjoys pursuing those interests in his spare time. He lives in Buffalo, New York.